Praise for *Sales 2.0*

"As founder of Oracle's telephone sales group, Anneke Seley pioneered today's modern selling techniques."

—Marc Benioff, Founder and CEO, salesforce.com

"Sales 2.0 is a major trend that is approaching the tipping point. Seley and Holloway have written the rare business strategy book that is immediately actionable. It's mandatory reading for sales professionals and business leaders alike."

—Geoffrey Moore, Best-Selling Author of *Crossing the Chasm,*
Dealing with Darwin, and other books

"Anneke has been an innovator in maximizing the efficiency and effectiveness of sales organizations, from the introduction of telesales channels to Web 2.0 communities, and has dramatically improved the way business is done."

—Craig Conway, Former CEO, PeopleSoft

"The authors have been at the forefront of creating and defining the Sales 2.0 phenomenon and show you how to make money and achieve exceptional ROI with this approach."

—John Luongo, Former CEO, the Vantive Corporation

"No sales executive wakes up and says 'How do I reach more customers in a more expensive way?' Implementing strategies and technologies that allow you to be more competitive is the key to success. If you are concerned with long-term success and viability of your organization and maintaining the pulse of your customer, you must read this book."

—Rudy Corsi, Senior Vice President, OracleDirect and Operations,
Oracle Corporation

"As a former Sales 1.0 professional, I can vouch for the fact that Sales 2.0 works. Since adopting a Sales 2.0 approach to selling, I have achieved increases in quota attainment as well as predictability in sales forecasts."

—Stu Schmidt, Vice President of Solutions Sales, Cisco WebEx

SALES 2.0

IMPROVE BUSINESS RESULTS USING INNOVATIVE SALES PRACTICES AND TECHNOLOGY

Anneke Seley
Brent Holloway

WILEY

John Wiley & Sons, Inc.

Published by John Wiley & Sons, Inc., Hoboken, New Jersey.
Published simultaneously in Canada.

For general information on our other products and services or for technical support, please contact our Customer Care Department within the United States at (800) 762-2974, outside the United States at (317) 572-3993 or fax (317) 572-4002.

Wiley also publishes its books in a variety of electronic formats. Some content that appears in print may not be available in electronic books. For more information about Wiley products, visit our web site at www.wiley.com.

Library of Congress Cataloging-in-Publication Data:

Seley, Anneke, 1958–
    Sales 2.0 : improve business results using innovative sales
practices and technology / Anneke Seley, Brent Holloway.
        p. cm.
    Includes bibliographical references and index.
    ISBN 978-0-470-37375-0 (cloth)
        1. Selling—Data processing.   2. Selling—Technological innovations.   3. Sales management—Technological innovations.   I. Holloway, Brent, 1974–   II. Title.
    HF5438.35.S453   2009
    658.85—dc22

                                                                        2008029060

Printed in the United States of America.

10 9 8 7 6 5 4 3 2 1

This book is dedicated to our customers, who have rewarded our Sales 2.0 philosophy with their business and shown that it works.

CONTENTS

ACKNOWLEDGMENTS

W e learned a great deal in the course of writing this book, thanks to the many people who were willing to help. Like Sales 2.0, this project is a result of collaboration and idea sharing.

Jeff Weinberger started as a business contact at Cisco WebEx, but quickly became an intellectual guide and good friend. He spent many hours reviewing, editing, and helping us think about Sales 2.0 as well as authoring our Afterword.

Anneke's team at Phone Works—especially Sally Duby, Cathie Dodge, Charissa Franklin, Anita Gryska, and Leslie Rearte—edited our drafts and gave us important perspectives. B. J. Bushur, our partner and friend, introduced us to Syneron and other customers featured in the book. Thanks to Hank Oswald as well, for being a willing member of the review team.

Sherry Paterra provided important guidance for this project. A friend, mentor, and early Sales 2.0 business leader, she helped with everything from strategic thinking to line-by-line editing.

Aaron Ross made major contributions to the manuscript. We are so grateful to have collaborated with him, so his experiences could be shared.

Without Barry Trailer's and Jim Dickie's CSO Insights research, the book's message would be much less compelling.

Lauren Hauptman gave us the confidence that only a professional editor can provide with her generous review of major sections. Ken Fromm, an author and entrepreneur, also gave us valuable ideas on how to improve the work.

Dave Thompson and his team at Genius.com gave Sales 2.0 early visibility and brought the pioneers of the Sales 2.0 community together with the inaugural Sales 2.0 Conference in 2007.

Geoffrey Moore sparked the idea for the Sales 2.0 conference. He also graciously agreed to be a part of this book as the author of its Foreword.

Barry Trailer, Vance Christensen, and Tina Babbi saw early outlines for the book and helped us rework its focus. The result is a much higher-quality product.

Lisa Herling educated Anneke on the world of professional publishing. Her network led to a referral to John Willig, who became our literary agent.

John Willig introduced us to Matthew Holt, our executive editor at John Wiley & Sons, and helped us convince him that a book on Sales 2.0 was a good investment.

The Wiley team has been wonderfully supportive. Without Matthew Holt's approval of the project, and Jessica Campilango's assistance throughout the process, there would be no book. Christine Moore, our developmental editor, read all our ugly first drafts and made the content crisper. Christine Kim, our marketing manager, helped us with our promotional questions and projects.

Ellie Koss, Brian Anderson, Bill Concevitch, Barry Trailer, Aaron Ross, Sramana Mitra, Mike Saylor, Dave Green, and many others gave us early advice and encouragement on writing, editing, publishing, and the creative process.

Kathleen Bruno, Jennifer Brandenburg, and Frances Evensen made vital introductions to many of the key people featured in our interviews. Relationships matter!

Many generous people agreed to be interviewed or quoted for the book. We enjoyed each and every interaction, although not everyone's stories could be told. We appreciate the time they spent with us and are grateful for their participation.

We thank our sales managers, not only for providing encouragement and content for this project, but also for teaching us about sales and sales management. The career opportunities and guidance they provided have given us the credibility to write this book. Anneke is especially indebted to Craig Conway, Mike Seashols, John Luongo, Tom Siebel, and Mike Humphries. Anneke also thanks Larry Ellison for hiring her in the early days of Oracle and Marcia Wells-Lawson, her first manager, for patiently teaching her the basics of business. Brent thanks Doron Aspitz, Jeff Schmidt, Roger Nunn, Brian Anderson, Omar Kassem, Gary Trudo, Brad Mirkovich, and Bill Ryan for their leadership as innovative sales managers.

Writing a book can be an emotional roller coaster. Our spouses bore the brunt of this and made it possible for us to deliver the manuscript within our short, five-month deadline. Anneke thanks Jack Oswald for urging her to write a book in the first place and reminding her on a constant basis of the strategic value and timeliness of the Sales 2.0 message. His insights helped shape the book and make it pertinent and actionable for executives and business leaders. Brent thanks his wife, Cindy Holloway, for her ongoing support and encouragement.

PREFACE

I n 1876, Alexander Graham Bell's invention of the telephone provided the first technological alternative to information exchange
by mail or in person. In more recent times, we have access to a
dazzling array of online products, mobile devices, and automated
services that are changing the way we communicate and, therefore,
how customers buy and how sellers sell. However, despite more than a
century of technological advancement, we still have sales productivity
challenges.

Thought leaders and technology vendors are defining a phenomenon called Sales 2.0, which evokes a newer, better, more effective
way to identify and communicate with customers. Like Web 2.0—
which defines the Internet as the platform for creating new business
opportunities—Sales 2.0 is an umbrella term for describing best practices for predictable, measurable selling that results in improved business
results. Although the "2.0" version number suggests that the Internet-
based sales enablement tools are what give companies a performance
edge, Sales 2.0 is not just about the Internet and the technological
advances of Web 2.0. Technology, in fact, is *enabling* the Sales 2.0
movement—which centers on a measurable, customer-centric sales process, strong and aligned relationships, and the strategic application of
sales resources for maximum profitability.

This book's purpose is to demystify the emerging Sales 2.0 trend and
present ideas on how you can profit from it. We provide a framework for
business leaders and sales professionals to understand the many facets
of Sales 2.0 from the perspective of experienced sales managers. Since

change in general is difficult, and implementing Sales 2.0 requires a different mindset, we provide guidance on how to introduce Sales 2.0 to your organization to achieve lasting success. Throughout the book, we demonstrate how Sales 2.0 leads to better business results in the real world, which transforms this subject from an academic curiosity to a compelling business case.

In Part 1, we introduce you to the general concepts of Sales 2.0 and its importance to your company. We explain why changing the way you sell is imperative, and we cover some common misperceptions that hinder the process of reaping the benefits of Sales 2.0. Part 2 explores the Sales 2.0 practice of selling by telephone and Web and shows how inside sales is a strategic entry point and baseline for future Sales 2.0 initiatives. Part 3 showcases four innovative companies that are using Sales 2.0 practices to create competitive advantage and impressive returns. In Part 4, we conclude with some practical approaches to getting started with Sales 2.0—including illustrations of how companies are using technology products to support the sales practices that improve business results.

The Sales 2.0 strategy includes the proper alignment of sales and marketing and well as sales resources and customer opportunities to create a leveraged approach to salesforce deployment and territory coverage. This means segmenting sales process steps, customers, and opportunities, and using the most profitable sales channel or communications medium needed to engage more buyers. Companies that include inside sales—the use of the telephone and Web to communicate with customers—in their sales mix, therefore, have a competitive advantage. Furthermore, companies gain the most traction and acceptance for Sales 2.0 practices through the groups that are most process-driven, technologically oriented, and open to change: inside sales groups for sales development and telesales. Through implementation of Sales 2.0 in sales development (for lead generation and qualification) and telesales (for telephone and web-based selling), companies can spearhead the transformation of an entire multichannel sales organization.

We pioneered Sales 2.0 concepts in the inside sales groups that we created and managed in the 1980s and 1990s, and we continue to perfect these approaches in our roles today. Although the quality and quantity of enabling technology products have increased by an order of magnitude, the fundamental sales practices have not changed. Using the phone and Web in the sales process is a huge opportunity for companies that have yet to fully exploit these highly effective, low-cost media, given shifts in customer buying preferences. For many businesses or markets, economics mandate the use of inside sales as the primary sales channel.

For nearly 20 years after leaving Oracle, Anneke has been applying the best sales practices she learned there and improving on them in the work she does with the clients of Phone Works, her sales consulting company. Led by her former Oracle colleague Sally Duby, the team of Phone Works consultants has designed, implemented, and relaunched measurable and predictable sales teams for hundreds of clients. Anneke has learned through her experiences that inside sales is a strategic business element and competitive differentiator with enormous value; and this book reveals why.

Brent has worked as a practicing sales manager with high-growth software companies for over 10 years. He is constantly looking for ways to increase the productivity of his telesales team at Verint Systems, which generates millions of dollars per year by staying engaged with customers. Brent writes on the topic of inside sales from a true insider's point of view. His research and reporting on implementing Sales 2.0 people, process, and technology focuses on measurable results in groups such as the one he himself manages.

Because of our job experiences and the companies with whom we've worked, the book highlights technology companies selling business-to-business (B2B)—complex products that typically require several interactions between customers and salespeople before a purchase is made. And although you may be thinking that Sales 2.0 only applies to Silicon Valley companies in the computer software and technological products industries, this is not at all the case. As Professor Andrew McAfee at Harvard Business School states in his blog ("The Pursuit of Busyness," *http://blog.hbs.edu/faculty/amcafee*, April 14, 2007), "I often look to high-tech companies to observe state of the art work practices. Something about the intensity of both the competition and the war for talent in their industries makes them laboratories for workplace innovations." This speaks directly to the fact that there is an important message here for readers in other industries with similarly complex sales cycles and evolving markets in which customers are using technology to communicate.

We've also discovered that Sales 2.0 practices can be applied more widely than we originally realized. Through discussions with professionals who are not in technology sales—including a cofounder of a prominent San Francisco Bay Area environmental nonprofit, and a medical entrepreneur who wants to transform the way health care is delivered—we have learned that Sales 2.0 approaches will likely yield improvements in all kinds of organizations, given the key concepts of functional and strategic resource alignment, measurable and predictable process, and online engagement.

We'd like to hear about your experiences with Sales 2.0, and share our ongoing insights after this book is published. Let's be consistent with the Sales 2.0 message, start a conversation online, and keep the relationship going! Join us on *www.sales20book.com*.

Thanks so much for reading our book.

FOREWORD

We are in the early stages of a movement called Sales 2.0. Forward-thinking companies are the practitioners of Sales 2.0, and technology vendors are supplying the tools to enable its practice. Sales 2.0 companies are experimenting with innovative sales practices every day in a changing world of customer preferences

Why implement Sales 2.0 now? Because it allows companies to win more deals faster. It creates low-latency sales cycles, prioritizes best sales opportunities, highly leverages scarce expertise, proliferates best practices, and provides an on-ramp for next-generation talent.

How is Sales 2.0 a whole new ball game? It requires a major shift in sales management style. It's all about measurement, tracking a sales team's performance and metrics-oriented management philosophy. For sales reps, it requires a light touch and the right touch—being at the right place at the right time for your customer with the right information. Sales 2.0 tools can help achieve this.

Sales 2.0 is also about being authentic, not the stereotypical hype-y salesperson. Sales 2.0 reps help your customer to buy as opposed to "selling them." The reward for Sales 2.0 selling is your customer's loyalty and business.

The bottom line? As a result, of "No pushing!" "less friction!" and "less fiction!" you will see "more action!" and "more traction!"

—GEOFFREY MOORE
Best-selling author, Managing Director at TCG
Advisors and Venture Partner at MDV

PART 1

Selling In The Twenty-First Century

1. What is Sales 2.0?
2. Why is Sales 2.0 Imperative for Your Business?
3. Sales 1.0 to Sales 2.0: Changing Mindset
4. Sales 2.0 Results and Rewards
5. Seven Misperceptions about Sales 2.0
6. Eight Sales 2.0 Imperatives
7. R U Sales 2.0? A Checklist

HOW INNOVATIVE SELLING BEGAN IN SILICON VALLEY

In the 1970s, IBM was the company to emulate in high technology. IBM's salespeople were considered the best in the business. Their image—symbolized by the dress code of dark business suits with nicely pressed white shirts and ties—was the height of professionalism. IBM's customer service and sales training program were legendary. Sales professionals like Mike Seashols, who started his career in sales at IBM, were highly regarded and sought-after for top jobs across the technology industry. Seashols was recruited to head Oracle's sales organization during the company's high-growth years of the 1980s and currently serves as chairman and CEO of Avolent. As an IBM sales professional, he virtually lived with his customers, one of whom was Steve Jobs; he spent more time at their offices than his own to make sure they received instant attention and were completely satisfied with IBM's products. Customers responded well to this level of service and rewarded IBM with their orders. It was said that "nobody ever got fired for buying Big Blue."

In the days before the advent of the personal computer and the commercial use of the Internet, computers cost hundreds of thousands of dollars and required large, dedicated, temperature-controlled rooms, and staffs of technical people to keep them running. Software, which cost tens of thousands to millions of dollars to license, was sold top down to what we now call the chief information officer (CIO)—the head of information technology—and approved by senior management. It was distributed on physical reels of magnetic tape and procured as a perpetual use license, personally delivered and installed at the customer's site by a technical specialist or team and carefully monitored until the application went live and was stable. Software upgrades also required onsite installation by a technical expert.

Mike Seashols remembers, "A typical IBM sales cycle was 12 months or longer. Sales reps usually made four sales calls to customers each day, two in the morning and two in the afternoon after lunch." Often, multiple meetings were required to close a sale, given the large financial investment required, the levels of customer management needed for approval, and the evangelical type of selling required to educate customers on new products. Lengthy contract negotiations were often needed as well before products were sold. Legal departments and contract administrators on both sides of the table could add weeks to the sales cycle, just to fulfill their responsibility to protect their company's interests and secure the best possible terms.

Due to the high costs associated with these installations, only the largest companies and government agencies could afford such expenditures. And these customers expected not only dedicated technical resources—which ensured smooth and successful implementations—but also perks that added to the cost of doing business. Customers often enjoyed invitations to expensive meals or rounds of golf, accompanied by their salesperson. As a result, technology vendors' cost of selling and servicing customers was so high and sales rep productivity was so limited that only the largest deals and biggest customers could be targeted in order to make a healthy profit.

Those were the good old days of Sales 1.0 selling in Silicon Valley. Boy, has the world changed.

In the mid-1980s, as computers became smaller, more affordable, and more ubiquitous, the market blew wide open for a much bigger range of less expensive software and hardware that appealed to a bigger universe of potential customers. No longer were these complex products the domain of only the *Fortune* 1000 and big government. The super-high-touch, labor-intensive way we used to sell technology products no longer made economic sense for markets, customers, or products requiring a high volume of sales transactions. Sales strategies and distribution channels in Silicon Valley had to evolve.

The old way of selling wasn't a fit for the new buyers either. Customers with smaller computers became more self-sufficient and often installed their own software without involving their information technology (IT) departments or requiring CIO or senior management approval. Contracts for smaller systems were initially simplified and shrink-wrapped with the product, which was shipped on discs. This approach made the negotiation of terms between legal departments increasingly rare. When it became possible to license software over the Internet, many software products became available for download through a web site link, and users would just check the "Accept" box online to agree to contractual terms. The simplification of the shipping, installation, and contractual requirements also reduced sales-cycle lengths and cost of sales and paved the way for much more software to be sold.

One could argue that the telephone was the first Sales 2.0 disruptive technology to be integrated into the sales process, as Oracle found in 1985. Under certain circumstances, prospects proved to be comfortable interacting with salespeople and even buying complex technology—such as packaged software—from them by phone, as long as they could get quick, accurate answers to their questions and discuss how a product could meet their business requirements. They often had the decision-making and budget authority for smaller purchases, and many preferred the efficiency and instant gratification of phone communication to the lengthy process and delays of scheduling onsite meetings. Trial license programs with liberal return policies preceded the downloadable demos and trials that are offered through many software vendors' web sites today.

The comfort level associated with this manner of buying products along with a thirst for purchasing them more efficiently has expanded to include bigger-ticket items with more complex sales cycles in technology—as well as in other industries. As our customers change, companies that are open, flexible, and changing the way they sell are creating competitive advantage, and leaving behind those that don't do so.

This new, emerging framework for selling effectively in the twenty-first century is called Sales 2.0.

1
WHAT IS SALES 2.0?

Sales 2.0 is the use of innovative sales practices, focused on creating value for both buyer and seller and enabled by Web 2.0 and next-generation technology. Sales 2.0 practices combine the science of process-driven operations with the art of collaborative relationships, using the most profitable and most expedient sales resources required to meet customers' needs. This approach produces superior, predictable, repeatable business results, including increased revenue, decreased sales costs, and sustained competitive advantage.

THE FOUNDATION OF SALES 2.0

The innovations associated with Sales 2.0 practices fit into four inter-related, interdependent categories: strategy, people, process, and technology (Figure 1.1). Sales 2.0 organizations feature:

1. *Strategy* which includes alignment of sales resources with customer opportunities and leverages your most expensive professionals while providing coverage for buyers regardless of location, size,

Figure 1.1   The Foundation of Sales 2.0

or stage in the sales cycle. Sales 2.0 companies also have the right go-to-market plan and integrated, coordinated sales and marketing plans.

2. *People* who are relationship-focused, open, authentic, and flexible. They create and maintain collaborative interactions with people both inside and outside the company, using the most appropriate medium to engage and maintain relationships. Sales 2.0 professionals are trusted and enjoy support from customers, partners, colleagues, and peers alike, which leads to improved business results for all parties.

3. *Process* that is customer-focused, measurable, reproducible, and automated, and which can be duplicated across a sales organization to produce predictable sales results from quarter to quarter. The Sales 2.0 process results in optimized sales efficiency and effectiveness, and ultimately high-velocity, high-volume, and high-value transactions. Deals close faster, there are more of them, and they are more profitable.

4. *Technology* which enables sales process and relationship-building, and which helps your people be more productive and successful.

Sales 2.0 Strategy: Alignment and Resource Allocation

Sales 2.0 businesses perform market analysis to identify customer types and requirements and assign the most profitable sales resources appropriate for each customer segment and market. Your most experienced and expensive sales teams should be focused on your largest qualified customers or sales opportunities. You can leverage their time and attention with a sales strategy that includes sales resources dedicated to sales opportunities that do not require face-to-face interaction. This includes qualifying buyers of all sizes in early stages of your sales cycle, smaller sales opportunities or prospects that may be geographically distant, and customers who have already purchased products from you. These communities can often be served by lower-cost sales resources using the phone and online technology. Sales 2.0 strategy leverages the most expensive sales reps while keeping sales pipelines consistently full, increasing customer acquisition and revenue generation, which keeps cost of sales low to deliver maximum value to investors and shareholders.

Sales and marketing alignment is especially important in Sales 2.0. These departments function together as one continuum to generate interest and engage customers. They collaborate on key strategy decisions as well as customer acquisition and relationship-building programs. Without the right go-to-market strategy, companies cannot enjoy Sales 2.0 benefits. These strategic prerequisites include product offering, positioning, messaging, pricing, target audience and qualified lead definitions, and channel distribution appropriate for the customers in your market. Without getting these right, Sales 2.0 initiatives—and Sales in general—will be ineffective. Although this book does not address these preconditions for success—numerous other books explore these marketing fundamentals in great detail—we do cover Sales 2.0 practices that can be used to test and refine or correct your marketing and sales strategies.

Sales 2.0 People: Open, Flexible, Collaborative, and Tech-Savvy

Relationships, interaction, and collaboration among different constituencies are major themes in Sales 2.0. The main selling relationship focus is on the connection between sales reps and their prospects or customers. As time progresses, the majority of these interactions are occurring by phone and Web. In addition, teamwork among colleagues is another prerequisite for Sales 2.0 success. The aforementioned sales and marketing alignment is a classic example of a Sales 2.0 relationship, and with technology, the line between the two functions is blurring. Also, close collaboration between inside and field reps, sales reps and sales support staff such as subject matter experts (SMEs), and contracts or legal leads to shorter sales cycles and increased revenue in Sales 2.0 companies.

In order to achieve Sales 2.0 levels of relationships and collaboration, company cultures will inevitably shift and managers may need to rethink their hiring strategies and compensation plans for sales employees. This new breed of sales rep must be open to change in the sales profession. As they focus on building relationships with customers and peers, these open-minded reps use the phone and Web extensively in place of on-site visits to contain costs, improve productivity, and provide more immediate service. They need to come up to speed on new technologies as customers adopt them. These Sales 2.0 reps often have team-selling goals—in addition to individual ones—that are supported by compensation plans that reward Sales 2.0 behavior. And for maximum performance gains, they must embrace a sales process that evolves with changing customer and market conditions.

Sales 2.0 Process: A Customer-Centric Yardstick for KPIs (Key Performance Indicators)

Salespeople take certain steps to advance a sale, and their prospective customers take parallel steps to make a purchase decision. Sales 2.0 process is designed with customers at the forefront and asks: What are their business initiatives? What actions must they take at each step? What do they need from you and by when? Are you easy to do business with? This customer-focused process gives you a framework by which to measure your business metrics and key performance indicators (KPIs): to figure out what's working and what's not. Without it, you can't predict business results; nor can you duplicate successes by sharing knowledge and best practices, fine-tune your sales approaches when markets and customers' businesses change, or make continuous improvements as you experiment with different sales and marketing programs. Think of Sales 2.0 process measurement as part yardstick, part crystal ball.

Sales 2.0 Technology: The Right Tools for Your Sales Reps and Customers

The predictability, constant improvement in business processes, and strong, engaged online relationships that are the hallmarks of Sales 2.0 are supported by technology. It may be customer relationship management (CRM), business analytics, e-mail and web site tracking software; or products that accelerate account research or lead generation that help make sales reps more effective and efficient. Or it may by video e-mail, webinar software, or sales portals that encourage interaction, collaboration, and engagement. Without today's technology enabling detailed sales process measurement and analysis—as well as the meaningful building of relationships without in-person meetings—Sales 2.0 simply wouldn't be possible.

Recognizing the opportunity to enable these practices—which result in improved sales metrics—technology vendors have responded with an explosion of available online products. In general, these are Web 2.0 or advanced technologies that include software and services that speed up, enhance, or provide visibility into the sales cycle, or improve customer experience and engagement. In Part 4, we cover some of these technologies and how they are improving sales productivity.

Later in Part 1, we discuss eight imperatives for Sales 2.0 strategy, people, process, and technology in more detail. But first, we want to address some questions that may be on your mind:

☐ Why is it so important to begin a transformation to Sales 2.0?
☐ What happens if you don't?
☐ What do you need to change from the way you're selling now?
☐ What are the rewards for implementing Sales 2.0?

2

WHY IS SALES 2.0 IMPERATIVE FOR YOUR BUSINESS?

You may be asking, "Is Sales 2.0 really that important? Can my business survive without it?" In Part 3 of this book, we show you how four forward-thinking companies are leading their industries with Sales 2.0 practices. But they're not the only ones. Your competitors may be considering similar sales approaches—that is, if they haven't implemented Sales 2.0 already. Wouldn't you like to beat them to it?

The way we've been selling in the past is too expensive, too slow, too unpredictable, and too hazardous to relationships for today's businesses and their customers. Change is mandatory for those companies that want to outperform the competition. It is much more challenging to sell in today's world, where sales reps struggle to meet the increasing demands of their customers while keeping sales numbers high and expense dollars low. Sellers often contend with decentralized customer organizations, multiple decision makers, and complex decision-making processes. New competitors seem to enter the market every day, requiring ever-improving differentiation in products and services. Meanwhile buyers are on information overload and face a myriad of product offerings and multiple choices of vendors—not to mention a steady stream of marketing and advertising campaigns coming at them through multiple media.

Marketing and sales professionals in every industry need to re-examine their markets, potential new customers, and how new and current customers evaluate and select products. They need to adapt their marketing strategies and sales processes to match the way that *all* their customers want to buy, while maintaining the flexibility to allow different customers to buy in different ways. For many companies with complex, business-to-business (B2B) sales models—where competition has increased and technology advances have changed customer preferences—the traditional sales approaches that have yielded success in the past will not work for much longer. These models typically center on field-based sales reps and executives who conduct most of their business through face-to-face prospect and customer meetings, and who are accountable for the entire sales process from prospect to qualified lead to opportunity development to sale. These Sales 1.0 salesforces:

- ☐ Favor information control over facilitating customer self-service.
- ☐ Are more oriented to internal competition than team collaboration.
- ☐ Are not measured on anything but the short-term revenue they generate.
- ☐ Are focused on making quota this quarter without regard for making their customers successful over the long term and contributing profit to two bottom lines: their company's and their customer's.

These characteristics are endemic in Sales 1.0 organizations, many of which are already experiencing a slowdown in success.

KEY FACTORS DRIVING SALES 2.0 ADOPTION

There are seven significant factors that make it imperative for your business to implement Sales 2.0 practices to create sustainable advantage over your competition and create value for you and your customer, ensuring that when the dust settles, your company comes out on top. These factors are:

1. Customers' changing communications preferences.
2. Shifting power from sales reps to customers.
3. Rising cost of sales.
4. Customer demand for corporate social responsibility.
5. Different markets, different economics.
6. Decreasing sales effectiveness.
7. Increased customer demand for trust, responsiveness, and authenticity.

Customers' Changing Communications Preferences

In the 1980s, e-mail and web sites were not yet part of everyday life. Businesses routinely mailed documents such as brochures or contracts—or shipped them overnight in urgent situations. Toward the end of the decade, a new technology—the fax machine—allowed us to share printed or visual information faster.

Since those days, an evolution in communications and information access has been taking place in our society. Both at home and at work, we are embracing all kinds of technology to stay in touch and stay informed. E-mail, web sites, texting, instant messaging (IM), FaceBook, and YouTube are among the products and methods that have become an integral part of our everyday lives.

As a result, the way we buy and sell products is changing as well. Customer communications preferences have radically transformed in the last decade, and they will continue to do so as new technologies are released and become ubiquitous.

Relationships between sellers and buyers can be increasingly initiated, strengthened, and maintained online and by telephone, rather than in face-to-face meetings. Customers who need to interact with a salesperson before making a purchase decision are becoming very comfortable doing so by phone or Internet, given the powerful array of web-based tools available to fully demonstrate a product's capabilities.

Even if you haven't experienced these shifting communications preferences in your customer community yet, change is inevitable over time. The next generation of young people is growing up in a technological age, almost exclusively using applications such as MySpace, chat, and mobile-phone texting to communicate. Soon enough, this generation will be entering the workforce and becoming buyers and sellers—and with them, even the landline phone and e-mail are in danger of becoming outdated forms of information exchange. As customer landscapes change and buyer needs, communications preferences, and buying processes evolve, businesses need to prepare for change to respond accordingly.

Shifting Power from Sales Reps to Customers

Decades ago, customers had limited ability to access product information without seeing a salesperson. These salespeople were often aggressive, lone wolf road warriors who traveled door to door or consulted the Yellow Pages to find buyers. They brought their brochures and binders to three-martini lunches and spouted their product features and benefits in hopes that the customer would buy.

Not anymore. Sales reps have evolved from information sources to solutions consultants. Given today's technology, salespeople can no longer realistically control information; prospects go online to research product solutions before ever engaging with a salesperson. Company- and vendor-independent web sites provide countless tools such as videos, podcasts, free demos, and recorded webinars that provide information on demand 24 hours a day. Prospects and customers are becoming more and more educated about the companies and people from whom they buy. Through social networks and community sites, they can tap into personal connections for references as well as both good and bad product reviews. Every day, customers are increasing their sophistication and using technology to empower their decision making.

Fortunately, buyers and sellers have similar goals: Customers want easy and expedient access to product and company information, and sales teams want information on their prospects' business initiatives. Buyers like to find the easiest, most appropriate solution to their particular needs in the shortest amount of time; sellers constantly aim to shorten their sales cycles. Prospects seek vendors who understand and can solve their problems quickly; sales reps' goals are to find the prospects that are the most qualified to buy. Customers are looking for trusted partner relationships with their sales counterparts, excellent customer service, and influence on future product and service direction, and sales professionals seek long-term relationships with happy clients who become repeat customers and great references. Everyone wants to improve productivity, increase trust, strengthen relationships, and ultimately, maximize business results.

Consequently, customers and salespeople alike are gravitating to new selling and buying strategies and technologies that improve the efficiency and effectiveness of their buying and selling experiences. Customers are rewarding companies who choose to employ the innovative sales practices of Sales 2.0 with their initial and repeat purchases.

Rising Cost of Sales

Yes, the cost of fuel is at an all-time high, but out-of-control sales expense is not just a function of travel-related costs. Companies that don't leverage their sales resources and improve sales productivity waste precious time and money. The ever-rising cost of sales—a prominent item on company expense budgets—is forcing businesses to reevaluate distribution models and improve sales effectiveness. It is simply too expensive—in terms of the travel and entertainment budget, as well as your sales reps' time—to visit every customer every time a meeting is needed. Companies with lengthy sales cycles, unreliable forecasts, and low customer retention rates are looking for ways to decrease their sales costs by improving sales results and return on investment (ROI). In the face of change, some business requirements remain constant: making quarterly revenue and profit numbers, maintaining competitive advantage, growing market share, and delivering value to your investment community.

Customer Demand for Corporate Social Responsibility

On top of the financial expense of airplane and car travel, these modes of transportation have environmental costs that can harm your reputation and make you unattractive as a vendor. Sustainability is an urgent issue for customers around the world, and socially sensitive companies are implementing innovative ways to reach out and respond to them without the high financial and societal costs of using transportation fuel. IBM's Global CEO Study, "CEO's Battle to Keep Up with the Pace of Change" (based on interviews with 1,130 CEOs and business and public-sector leaders from 40 countries, May 2008), reports that customers are now expecting their vendors to demonstrate corporate social responsibility, including the employment of green initiatives.

Different Markets, Different Economics

The economics of some markets and business models require the economies of scale that Sales 2.0 makes possible. Businesses that sell products to large, geographically dispersed markets—such as small and medium-size businesses (SMB)—will go broke trying to sell lower-priced products in high volume without a highly effective and efficient sales approach based on Sales 2.0 principles. Similarly, successful businesses that offer products or services on a subscription or on-demand basis—for instance, those that sell software as a service (SaaS)—have embraced Sales 2.0 as their primary selling mode in order to attract and retain large numbers of customers of all sizes. Because these companies typically sell their product or service repeatedly at high transaction rates, they rely on Sales 2.0 selling to produce a consistent revenue stream.

Decreasing Sales Effectiveness

The evidence is clear. The sales practices employed today by most organizations are no longer working. Though companies continue to rank increased revenue and improved sales effectiveness as top priorities year after year, research shows that by many measures, these objectives have not been attained. IDC—a global provider of market intelligence, advisory services, and events for the information technology, telecommunications, and consumer technology markets—reports that sales productivity is the number-one business initiative on CEOs' agendas (IDC QuickLook Survey, IDC's Enterprise Panel, January 2008). CSO Insights, a research firm that specializes in benchmarking the challenges that are having an impact on the performance of sales and marketing organizations, makes some surprising revelations in its annual surveys. The firm reports that the percentage of companies achieving their annual revenue targets has declined since 2005 across industries and in companies of all sizes. The average number of individual sales reps who miss their annual quota is close to 40 percent, and the ramp-up time for new reps has increased substantially since 2003 and earlier. In addition, forecast accuracy has declined for many years in a row (2008 Sales Performance Optimization Survey of over 1,500 companies on more than 100 metrics, by CSO Insights, *www.csoinsights.com*).

Increasing Customer Demand for Trust, Responsiveness, and Authenticity

Today's customers are faced with ever-increasing product choices and complexity. Their companies are hyper-focused on cost and ROI. As a result, their expectations of sales reps are changing. They are not looking for someone to take them out to lunch or buy them drinks in return for a fast order. They are instead seeking a trusted partner who really listens to their requirements, is easy to work with, and helps them meet their business objectives in a timely fashion. Clients expect vendors to be honest about what they can and can't deliver. They don't want to—and can't afford to—do business with companies that they never hear from once their order is placed.

IS TECHNOLOGY THE ANSWER?

Not by itself.

Technology vendors have embraced the term *Sales 2.0* to address sales challenges and describe a new and improved way of selling. Sales 2.0 technologies are so named because many incorporate Web 2.0 functionality, which emphasizes interaction, collaboration, and open sharing of information over the Internet. This rapidly growing category of products addresses age-old challenges that are associated with sales performance. These range from tracking, measuring, and analyzing sales activities and results, to improving or enabling certain parts of the sales cycle, to providing rich online communications vehicles for customers to research companies and interact with sales professionals. Given the multitude of challenges facing sales professionals today, technology companies are responding with products that can produce increased effectiveness and efficiency—both of which lead to improved sales performance.

While technology is a key component and major enabler of the Sales 2.0 phenomenon, it is not a universal panacea that automatically leads companies into sales nirvana. Technology vendors supply the tools that enable solutions; they do not provide the solutions in and of themselves. And unfortunately, many companies don't focus on the right things—sales rep and customer productivity and engagement—when implementing this technology. Gerhard Gschwandtner, Publisher of *Selling Power* magazine, claims that "sales leaders need to think harder about the effects of technology. Technology is like medicine; it has side effects that show up only after you've purchased and taken the medicine. We can't look at sales through the lens of technology; we need to look at technology through the lens of the customer."

You cannot simply implement technology and expect it to work on its own; rather, you begin by identifying your customers' buying processes and align your sales process accordingly. You must shift your point of view to that of your customers in order to integrate technology that works for everybody. Implementing the appropriate technology is required to achieve the sales productivity gains associated with the Sales 2.0 practices of sales process measurement, customer relationship management, and online customer engagement.

3
SALES 1.0 TO SALES 2.0: CHANGING MINDSET

The difference between Sales 1.0 and the new imperative of Sales 2.0 is more than just the definition of a sales process, the update of hiring profiles, and the implementation of some new technology. Jeff Weinberger, who oversees Cisco WebEx's Sales 2.0 initiative, underlines the importance of mindset in moving from the old world of Sales 1.0 and embracing the new imperatives of Sales 2.0. Jeff explains, "Sales 2.0 leaders think differently about building and structuring sales organizations. Making the shift from Sales 1.0 to Sales 2.0 won't be sustainable in your organization unless your leadership has begun to change its mindset and commits to the change."

In the next sections, we discuss the different perspectives required for your business to begin the evolution.

SALES IS ART AND SCIENCE

Veteran senior executive and former top-selling IBM sales rep of the 1970s Mike Seashols is a prime example of a Sales 1.0 superstar. Mike is a naturally talented sales professional who exudes charisma and has a gift for connecting with customers and employees. He admits, "I never needed a sales process; for me, it was intuitive." This is in keeping with a mindset that is prevalent in Sales 1.0: sales is an art. In many industries, executives hiring sales teams and managers place artistry and a winning personality at the top of their lists of qualifications for all of their sales candidates.

The Sales 1.0 belief that sales is largely an art form stands in stark contrast with the Sales 2.0 premise that the selling function can be made more scientific and predictable with Sales 2.0 practices. Although Mike Seashols exemplifies the Sales 1.0 artist, he recognized early in his career that art alone would not guarantee a sales organization's success. When he started managing other people, he recalls, "I needed to codify what I was doing at each step in the sales process, so I could ask my sales team to consistently follow my winning formula."

Some suggest that the analog of Sales 2.0 is a manufacturing conveyor belt. While this comparison is useful, it only goes so far. Sales involves communications and relationships between human beings; not interactions between machine parts. It is not merely a numbers game. Success in sales requires a combination of art and science. In Sales 2.0 terms, the art is forming strong customer relationships; the science is improving sales process and measurement.

Art, however—though useful on an individual sales rep level—is difficult to duplicate and scale across an operation. Sales art can be very powerful in establishing strong relationships and winning key sales, but it is unpredictable and unsustainable at the corporate strategy level. In their market research reports on sales effectiveness, Barry Trailer and Jim Dickie, partners at CSO Insights, reveal that the average results across organizations show that "the more you rely on the science of selling versus the art, the more success you will achieve." Building predictable sales processes is the first priority when implementing Sales 2.0. When you identify your star salespeople, you can figure out what makes them successful, build those practices into your process, and train everyone else on their approaches.

In Jim Collins's bestseller *Good to Great* and his accompanying web site (www.jimcollins.com), the author describes a concept called the flywheel as one of the requirements for achieving disciplined action and greatness. He writes, "We build greatness by a cumulative process—step by step, action by action, day by day, week by week, year by year—turn by turn of the flywheel." Through consistency, this flywheel gradually builds momentum and becomes an unstoppable force. Sales process can be the driver of this flywheel in your business.

THINKING LIKE YOUR CUSTOMER

We've all had frustrating experiences as customers. Horror stories abound concerning the awful price negotiation we have to endure to buy a new car, the endless time we have to spend on hold to buy an airline ticket, or the customer support now outsourced by many businesses to someone who can't solve our problem.

How much time have you spent viewing and evaluating your own company's sales process from the outside in? When you design your sales process around how your customer buys, you have to step into their shoes and think like they do. Once you transform your way of thinking and begin to truly understand your customers' experiences and perspectives, you'll begin to think like a Sales 2.0 professional.

THE EVOLUTION FROM SALES 1.0 TO SALES 2.0

Keeping in mind the importance of changing your mindset, let's take a look at how the evolution from Sales 1.0 to Sales 2.0 affects our strategy, people, process, and technology (Table 3.1).

TABLE 3.1   Sales 1.0 to Sales 2.0

	Sales 1.0	Sales 2.0
Strategy	High-cost sales resources for all opportunities	Leveraged sales organization focused on profitability
	Marketing versus sales: silos with different objectives	Integrated marketing and sales: both focused on customer engagement
	Field sales only (or dominant)	Field and phone/web (inside) sales work together
	Main market: large companies	Multiple markets: large companies and small and medium-size businesses (SMB)
People	Rely mostly on art	Rely on science and art
	Mostly face-to-face meetings	Extensive use of phone/web/technology
	Pitch features and benefits	Understand customer's business goals and help solve problems
	Sellers control buyer information	Buyers educate themselves
	Individual achievement only	Individual achievement + teams/sharing/collaboration/relationships
Process	None or poorly defined, inconsistent	Flexible and consistent
	Seller focused	Buyer focused
	Tracking, measurement focused on end-of-quarter (revenue) results	Constant tracking, measurement, testing, and refinement of the entire sales cycle
Technology	Customer Relationship Management (CRM)/Salesforce Automation (SFA) enable management reporting more than rep productivity and effectiveness	CRM + advanced Web 2.0 sales applications enable process and measurement, increase productivity, and enhance customer engagement
	E-mail, web sites, some sales applications but limited metrics tracking and online customer engagement	

4

SALES 2.0 RESULTS AND REWARDS

SALES 2.0 COMPANIES SEE BETTER RESULTS

> There is a compelling reason to plan a transformation from Sales 1.0 to Sales 2.0 now: *Sales 2.0 companies produce superior business results.*

The CSO Insights sales performance optimization report includes a Sales Relationship/Process (SRP) Matrix[TM], which shows that the best-performing sales organizations—as measured by key metrics such as the percentage of reps making quota, the percentage of overall company plan achieved, and the percentage of forecast deals won—are those with the best customer and prospect relationships and the most advanced use of consistent, yet flexible sales processes to maintain these trusted relationships. In Sales 2.0 terms, the best performers define and follow Sales 2.0 practices.

We describe those companies with low levels of process-implementing and relationship-building skills as Sales 1.0 and those with high levels as Sales 2.0 and view the CSO Insights data accordingly (Table 4.1).

TABLE 4.1 Performance Data Associated with Sales 1.0 and Sales 2.0 Practices

	Sales 1.0 Process and Relationships (%)	Sales 2.0 Process and Relationships (%)
Reps making quota	56	69
Company quota achieved	86	93
Forecasted deals won	44	55

Another indicator of a company's better-than-average sales performance is its use of the Internet to engage with customers—also a common Sales 2.0 practice. CSO Insights' data show that all surveyed companies' usage of the Internet in the sales function has increased substantially in recent years, and the top-performing 10 percent of their survey population had the very highest Internet-usage rates to support sales. Additionally, sales leaders who use Sales 2.0 process and metrics to manage their sales teams have better performance results than those who do not.

Customers are clearly responding positively to companies with a Sales 2.0 approach. These companies are making it easier for their clients to do business with them by recognizing customer preferences and priorities. Those businesses that score at the highest levels of customer engagement and continuously improve their processes are being rewarded with more revenue.

INVESTORS REWARD SALES 2.0 COMPANIES

In the start-up world of Silicon Valley, new companies with Sales 2.0 business plans are winning, too. Investment professionals are realizing that companies dedicated to Sales 2.0 practices have a better chance of succeeding than those that aren't. Ray Lane is Managing Partner at Kleiner, Perkins, Caufield, & Byers (KPCB), one of the best-known and well-respected venture capital firms in the world. KPCB's web site describes the company as "passionately committed to helping their portfolio companies succeed." Ray has a history of building out-standing companies. Before joining KPCB, he served as president and chief operating officer of Oracle Corporation. During his eight-year tenure, Oracle's revenues grew from $1 billion to over $10 billion. Before that, he was senior partner with Booz-Allen & Hamilton where he pioneered and led a worldwide consulting practice targeted at helping senior management achieve better results from information technology. Ray brings his extensive knowledge of sales strategy and technology-enabled selling to his role as a venture capitalist, providing funding and expertise to new startups. One of the companies formerly in his portfolio, Visible Path, helps businesses and application providers integrate social networking into the tools people use at work. Ray says, "We quickly identified that Visible Path needed to change its traditional enterprise selling model and redeploy its salesforce, using Sales 2.0 practices. The company added lower-cost Inside Sales resources, streamlined its sales cycle, closed more deals, and became more profitable." As a result, Visible Path had a successful exit; the company was acquired by Hoover's, Inc., a Dun & Bradstreet Company, in January 2008.

Gordon Ritter is a Founder and General Partner at Emergence Capital, another top Silicon Valley venture capital firm focused on investments in technology-enabled services. He knows how to spot winners; one of his investments was salesforce.com, the worldwide leader in on-demand customer relationship management (CRM) services. Ritter claims, "In addition to a compelling customer-value proposition, we really examine a company's ability to execute against a sales plan prior to adding them to our portfolio. We look for a predictable, scalable sales process that one would classify as Sales 2.0. When our management teams present a revenue and profit forecast, I want to know if it's based in reality. Those companies employing Sales 2.0 practices give me the confidence I need to provide initial funding as well as continued investment."

Nancy Schoendorf, General Partner at Mohr Davidow Ventures, is a proponent of the Sales 2.0 concepts of collaboration, connection, and communication. She says, "Traditional boundaries between work and home have blurred due to the Internet. Customers determine what technologies get adopted during the selling process. That's why I back innovative, Sales 2.0 companies that foster greater interaction and new ways to communicate with potential buyers, regardless of location."

Wall Street rewards Sales 2.0 companies as well. Public companies with predictable sales forecasts are generally favored over those who make promises they can't keep or whose results are wildly variable. The stock market doesn't like surprises, and stock prices typically reflect that. Just look at what happened to General Electric in the first quarter of 2008. Two weeks after CEO Jeff Immelt announced earnings that fell well short of expectations, the company experienced the biggest one-day sell-off of its shares in 20 years (*Wall Street Journal*, April 24, 2008).

There is clear evidence showing that companies employing Sales 2.0 practices are seeing better business results than companies still stuck in the Sales 1.0 world. Sales 2.0 companies outperform Sales 1.0 companies in terms of company revenue goals achieved, percentage of sales reps making quota, and forecasted deals closed. They also reap the ultimate benefit of stockholder and investor confidence.

5
SEVEN MISPERCEPTIONS ABOUT SALES 2.0

S ales 2.0 requires more than just setting up processes, amending sales profiles, and licensing sales enablement technology. It means adopting a different way of thinking about the sales effort and how you relate to your customers and prospects. In the following section, you'll see how your current perceptions might derail your efforts to reach a new level of sales effectiveness and how you can start to change the way you think.

There are numerous misperceptions that get in the way of companies' abilities to achieve Sales 2.0. Here are the seven most common ones.

Misperception 1: My Company Is Making Its Numbers and I'm Not Targeting Small Accounts. I Don't Need to Implement Sales 2.0.

The "If it ain't broke, don't fix it" mentality is dangerous in our rapidly changing world. While companies with high-volume markets have the most urgent needs to rethink their sales strategies, Sales 2.0 is not just for companies targeting small and medium-size businesses (SMB). The

Sales 2.0 process brings science, predictability, and business intelligence to sales, and Sales 2.0 engagement promotes better relationships with customers and colleagues. These strategic advantages for companies result in increased sales productivity. As your competitors embrace Sales 2.0 and implement more effective, more engaging, and more profitable forms of customer communications, you are putting your company at risk by settling for the status quo.

By running a small pilot program, you can experiment with Sales 2.0 programs in a way that's comfortable for your organization—without sacrificing your current revenue stream and existing pipeline. In Part 3, you can read about how Oracle and WebEx use Sales 2.0 practices to do business with large accounts as well as small using process-driven, dedicated Inside Sales groups to keep sales pipelines consistently full while focusing revenue-generating reps on the most profitable sales activities. Also, you can learn how Syneron implemented Sales 2.0 initiatives that were countercultural for its industry and secured competitive advantage as a result.

Misperception 2: I Don't Need a Formal Sales Process. If We Hire the Right Sales Talent, We Will Make Our Numbers.

The myth of perfect senior sales executives with special, irresistible customer mojo—who can get the company out of any difficult revenue situation with their charisma—is rampant. It is also hopelessly untrue. Relying on such individuals, with their Rolodexes or business books, to attract initial customers might pull you through your first few quarters, but it is impossible to scale and sustain that magical power across an organization consistently every quarter.

The typical sales organization is made up of a handful of superstars and a majority of hard-working average performers. Wouldn't it be nice to understand what makes up the special art of the high achievers and train the mere mortals on those practices? (Hint: it usually involves following a sales process; for the superstar, it may be intuitive rather than conscious.) In the majority of organizations, it doesn't do you much good if 5 percent of your sales organization is at

200 percent of quota if the remaining 95 percent are below 50 percent. The strengths of an individual salesperson—who can save the day at the end of the quarter by bringing in a multimillion-dollar deal—are less important over time than a sales team that shares best practices, follows proven processes, and consistently contributes. Predictable revenue streams can only be achieved with ongoing lead generation and customer engagement programs and consistent, measurable sales process.

Another side to this misperception is the notion that if you bring a large salesforce on board, your company will automatically make its numbers. Hiring a multitude of salespeople—*before* you understand your customer buying patterns and the sales process that makes sense—will simply result in burning through cash faster. Mark Leslie and Charles Holloway of the Stanford Business School have written about the Sales Learning Curve (*Harvard Business Review*, July 1, 2006), during which start-ups or companies entering new markets need to learn about their business before ramping up their salesforces. They identify three phases—initiation, transition, and execution—that call for different kinds and sizes of salesforces. In the initial or learning stage, sales reps are doing more market research than revenue generation and shouldn't have stringent quotas. When launching Sales 2.0 programs—like an improved sales process or a new Inside Sales group—a small, sophisticated sales team will test and discover key customer targets, their concerns, what really resonates with them, and the appropriate sales process for their buying process. Once you determine your process as well as positioning, key markets, and messages and can start to see predictable results from your sales and marketing efforts, you can set reasonable revenue expectations and sales quotas. Hiring too many sales reps without a sufficient number of qualified sales opportunities is just a recipe for disappointment and missed expectations. A predictable sales process and the revenue expectations it reveals should drive your staffing plan and budget and also help you determine your hiring profile for salespeople.

Keeping sales capacity at the right levels while you are testing new programs and setting realistic sales expectations with your board of directors and investors is critical. Many new products, sales initiatives, or executive teams have been shut down prematurely because they didn't deliver against unrealistic plans in the early quarters.

Misperception 3: My New Sales 2.0 Initiatives Will Improve Revenue Results this Month.

Culture change and the introduction of new sales approaches always take longer than you'd like. You can often see initial results within a quarter with pilot programs, but testing and refining programs and building processes that produce repeatable revenue takes time. While it's difficult to be patient when it comes to sales, it's essential to set realistic expectations, especially for senior management and your board.

When implementing new Sales 2.0 organizations such as Inside Sales, sales leaders often underestimate the time it takes for a new sales rep or team to come up to speed and make revenue contributions, especially when a company sells a complex product or set of products into a diverse customer base. We know from CSO Insights' reports that it's taking longer for reps to get to full productivity than it did before 2003, a factor that can substantially impact revenue results. This is reason enough to invest in and test the results of training, sales tools and technology, and retention programs. It also makes sense to follow the productivity metrics of new hires—as Genius.com, profiled in Part 3, does—to determine which reps are on track and which ones need additional help to ramp up quickly.

The same theory applies to the introduction of new Sales 2.0 technologies. The fact that many of these tools—especially those sold on demand—are easily installed and maintained and intuitive to learn somehow means to some sales managers that such tools will instantly increase revenue results. Even with the simplest of technology, sales reps have a learning curve. They'll need training on how and when to integrate new tools into their daily work for maximum benefit. Plus it will take some time to find the best use of technology in your sales process and your customers' buying process.

Misperception 4: It Is Unnecessary to Invest in My Sales 2.0 Implementation. By Bootstrapping and Keeping Marketing and Sales Support Expense Low, I'll Improve Financial Results.

Implementing Sales 2.0 initiatives takes time and resources away from your already busy staff. By hiring professional recruiters, trainers, and consultants who specialize in these programs, you will fast-track your success and avoid common pitfalls while keeping your people focused on their primary responsibilities: delivering this quarter's revenue.

We've also seen countless examples of companies that underinvest in the marketing required for Sales 2.0 success, and who pay the price in missed revenue numbers—especially in companies selling to high-volume markets. For most companies, it takes healthy marketing investments to properly position products, build awareness, and generate interest in your prospect community. WebEx, for example, spends about the same amount of money per SMB sales rep on marketing as they do on each rep's total compensation. Salespeople who have to do the bulk of their own lead generation and qualification are much less effective than those who have a steady stream of leads delivered to them.

When a company underinvests in strategy development, marketing, training, sales support, and lead generation, sales reps and managers have to pick up the slack in order to make quota, which inevitably takes time away from selling. Keep your sales team focused on revenue-generating activities by providing the right infrastructure and supporting programs.

Misperception 5: It Doesn't Make Sense to Standardize the Company on Sales Process. Sales Managers Have Their Own Preferences.

We've seen that companies with the best, most predictable sales performance do not promote a sales-process-du-jour philosophy, but instead follow proven, standardized, flexible sales process steps to engage with customers. In many company cultures, it is popular to let chief sales officers and key sales leaders—who may not be up to speed on Sales 2.0 practices—do their own thing. This approach includes making regional or individual decisions on sales strategy and process. Some start-ups resist implementing sales process before hiring a VP of sales because of the belief that talented, senior salespeople will reject process and systems in favor of their tried and true sales approaches powered by strong personal connections. Our experience shows, however, that the most effective sales leaders understand the strategic strength of a metrics and process-based sales function and are most attracted to companies with the foresight to implement a tested sales model early. When hired into these forward-thinking companies, they will be able to evaluate the company's strengths and areas for improvement based on their sales process metrics and get to work on building their organization, expanding sales opportunities, and improving results, rather than implementing the basics.

To reap the substantial rewards of adding science to your sales function, view the implementation of a company-wide, consistent Sales 2.0 sales process as a strategic decision at the senior management team level. However, if your company sells to multiple markets in which buying processes are different, you may have different selling processes for different kinds of customers. Companies that fail to take advantage of consistent sales process aligned to customer buying process will find themselves losing sales and market share.

Misperception 6: Sales 2.0 Engagement Is Impersonal. It Is Always Better to Meet Customers Face-to-Face, Not on the Web or Phone.

Sales 2.0 principles emphasize communicating with customers using the medium of *their* preference. Face-to-face selling still has a place in Sales 2.0. If your prospect requests a field visit and the opportunity size and qualification level of the account justify the expense, Sales 2.0 includes getting in the car or on an airplane. But with communications preferences changing, and online engagement tools becoming commonplace, fewer customers need in-person visits to feel comfortable in a buying situation.

Still, a vast number of companies and salespeople still believe that you can't sell to customers unless they are physically sitting in the same room. While some traditional businesses or particular accounts still require this approach, we now have countless examples of companies large and small—some of whom are profiled in this book—that have achieved stunning success launching or expanding their businesses without a field sales organization by using Sales 2.0 practices. Others have proven that online and phone communications can accelerate many steps in the sales cycle, particularly in the early lead qualification and post-initial-purchase stages. Many companies' sales and profit results can be improved when the most senior and expensive sales resources are leveraged by less expensive ones working with customers of all sizes in the earliest parts of the sales cycle or with the company's smallest customers or opportunities throughout the buying process. For example, far too many companies dispatch a field rep to see a prospective customer before the opportunity is properly qualified—a practice that results in the field rep wasting time with accounts that will never become customers.

The CEO of Genius.com, Dave Thompson, points out that as the MySpace generation is about to enter the workplace—and in the coming decades moves up the ladder to become decision makers—we'd better be prepared to deal with people who are more comfortable relating to you online. In Part 2, you'll learn more about how and why communicating with buyers and selling by phone and Internet works.

Misperception 7: Sales 2.0 Won't Work Outside the Technology Industry or in Countries Other than the United States.

Technology companies are a natural fit for Sales 2.0 and telephone, Web, and technology-based sales models. But innovative companies in other markets such as banking, finance, and pharmaceuticals have had similar success with process-driven, technology-enabled Sales 2.0–style selling for decades. Furthermore, if yours is one of the first businesses in your industry segment to implement a Sales 2.0 strategy, this position could work to your advantage in differentiating your company from the alternatives. (See Syneron's story in Part 3 as an example.)

Globalization has made anyone anywhere a potential customer. But in order to sell to a global market, we have to understand how the customers outside our own country buy, and then design our sales practices accordingly. Sales 2.0 is not a U.S.-only phenomenon. The very nature of Sales 2.0—including changing your mindset to something different from your own and corresponding via methods other than in-person meetings—makes it *especially* global-client friendly. Oracle, among other companies, has seen great success piloting and then rolling out Sales 2.0 approaches worldwide. Its North American OracleDirect operation is supported by a large group of sales development specialists in Bangalore, India. Read more about these global Sales 2.0 programs in Part 3.

6
EIGHT SALES 2.0 IMPERATIVES

The Sales 2.0 formula for success consists of:

Strategy using the most profitable sales resources for greater productivity and aligning sales with marketing and other departments.

+

Process to optimize effectiveness and efficiency, or the science of sales.
People who facilitate relationships, engagement, and collaboration with buyers as well as colleagues, peers, and partners to strengthen relationships, or the art of sales.

+

Technology to automate or support these sales practices.

=

Improved Business Results: Predictable, Repeatable, Scalable Sales

S trategic use of sales resources; a scalable, repeatable process; improved results; better predictability; stronger relationships; and more value for both you and your customer all lead to one simple conclusion: becoming a Sales 2.0 business is not just the idea of the week. It's the one thing you *must* do if your company is to survive and thrive in the new, customer-driven world.

To help you get started, here are eight key focus areas that we call the Eight Sales 2.0 Imperatives. The companies we reference to illustrate the imperatives are profiled in Part 3 of this book.

The eight Sales 2.0 imperatives are:

1. Plan and test Sales 2.0 initiatives, organize sales resources strategically, and get executive-level support.
2. Facilitate sales and marketing collaboration and alignment.
3. Define an improved sales process and commit to it.
4. Use the sales process strategically.
5. Create personalized, long-term, collaborative relationships with prospects and customers.
6. Facilitate team selling and best-practices sharing.
7. Revisit sales employee profiles.
8. Implement technology to improve results.

Imperative 1: Plan and Test Sales 2.0 Initiatives, Organize Sales Resources Strategically, and Get Executive-Level Support

You're ready to get started with Sales 2.0. But how? There are many aspects to Sales 2.0—addressing strategy, people, process, and technology—and it's easy to get overwhelmed. You can't do everything at once. It's a good idea to start with a plan and set priorities.

When you define your Sales 2.0 initiatives to transform your sales practices, set specific, measurable goals for sales-performance improvement—and get management on board with the program. Identify different customer types and sales-resource needs, and organize your salesforce accordingly. You'll likely want to use the most expensive sales channels for the highest-value opportunities and customers and lower-cost phone- and web-based channels when appropriate in the sales cycle. Set *realistic* expectations for budget and time frames that are required for results; remember that this isn't a process that can be put into action overnight. Whether you are implementing process, people, or technology changes, be sure to take some key sales-performance measurements (e.g., revenue and profit per sales rep, percentage of reps making quota, average selling price [ASP], average sales-cycle length) before and after your initiatives are put into place. Make sure your basic go-to-market strategy (e.g., product strategy, positioning, pricing) is sound.

Implement Sales 2.0 initiatives in phases rather than shocking your sales organization with multiple behavior changes at once. One company was so enthusiastic about adding Inside Sales to its channel mix that they started up three teams simultaneously, hired large numbers of reps, and ended up with a field sales organization that refused to work with the new organization. The company had to shut down the effort and start over with a small pilot program. As tempting as it may be to transform your sales organization overnight, it is usually a recipe for revolt and disaster. People need time to adjust to change. They need to see proof that a new way of doing things will produce hoped-for results. Whether you're introducing a formalized sales process for the first time, implementing an Inside Sales group, or testing a new technology, make changes incrementally and pilot the new concepts. As illustrated by the company profiles in Part 3, your best chance for success is by choosing pilot groups that are open to change and eager to improve.

See how the pilot works. You'll learn what works and what doesn't, and you'll have a chance to make corrections before rolling out the program to the entire sales organization. Often, the team most willing to experiment will be your best performers. Sales reps who are already overachieving appreciate the recognition as well as the opportunity to increase their earning potential even more. And the rest of the sales organization will adopt new methods more readily when they see the success of the pilot team, especially when it comprises top-selling reps.

As with any major organizational shift, give your employees enough time to adjust, especially when making territory or compensation changes. Provide initial and ongoing training for initiatives requiring new skills, such as new technology usage. When introducing the Sales 2.0 program rollout, do so with a lot of fanfare at a kick-off event such as a sales rally. This kind of occasion will build excitement and highlight the pilot results and future expectations associated with the program in terms of personal and company benefits, such as financial gain.

Sales 2.0 companies follow these strategies with great success:

- ☐ Oracle, WebEx, Syneron, and Genius.com all have Sales 2.0 cultures that are driven by executive-level support for their programs.
- ☐ Syneron took a four-phase approach to implementing new Sales 2.0 initiatives, which included revamped sales processes and two Inside Sales pilots that tested telephone relationship building with prospects and clients. At the conclusion, they not only had a better understanding of their business metrics, they also had a full pipeline of new opportunities and a field salesforce that was eager to work with the new inside groups.

Imperative 2: Facilitate Sales and Marketing Collaboration and Alignment

Customer relationships can make or break sales results. So can relationships among sales, marketing, and other departments in your company. Year after year, CSO Insights reports that one of the top sales-effectiveness priorities for chief sales officers (CSOs) is optimizing lead-generation programs. But in most companies, marketing departments are still frustrated by the lack of lead follow-ups by the salesforce; and sales still believes that marketing only delivers unqualified leads. Sales and marketing alignment is, therefore, a phenomenon that remains elusive.

Without achieving initial and ongoing agreement and collaboration between sales and marketing and having them agree on the right target customers—and then attract and nurture them with the messages and positioning appropriate for these customers—sales effectiveness will suffer. We've seen marketing departments that insist the CEO or a senior executive is the target audience for their product and direct all their programs to those individuals. However, sales reps find that these high-level contacts are unreachable and that they have better success talking to departmental managers. In situations like this, the sales function will have difficulty making its numbers.

In Sales 2.0 companies, sales and marketing have collaborative relationships: Marketing is dedicated to engaging prospective customers that sales needs to make quota, and they develop sales programs and tools that are helpful in starting conversations with customers. For their part, the sales team is committed to providing information on which marketing efforts generate the best leads and which messages and incentives are the most effective in conversations with buyers. Sales also follows up with qualified leads in a timely manner and provides closed-loop information on which prospects closed. Both marketing and sales are tuned in to online communities and networks where their prospects and customers may participate and are active themselves in those communities. Sales process metrics and data keep both functions accountable to each another.

Scoring leads may sound like a simple and tactical assignment. But one of the most common misalignments that occurs between marketing and sales stems from the lack of agreed-on definitions of the terms *target customer* and *qualified lead*. If marketing and sales have different ideas about the markets and types of customers that your company should be going after—and which ones are most qualified to buy—this will create ongoing friction between the groups. One of the best ways to surface this disconnect is by creating a lead ranking or grading system together. Once it's created and agreed to by all key parties in marketing and sales, you collectively decide upon the actions to take for each type of lead. For example:

☐ *A and B leads:* Dispatch immediately to the appropriate sales rep.
☐ *C leads:* Nurture through marketing programs such as outbound e-mail and phone campaigns.
☐ *D leads:* Remove from database or label as unqualified.

Through tracking and measuring the steps of the sales process, marketing departments in Sales 2.0 companies are better able to determine the effectiveness of their programs—not just in terms of numbers of prospects, but also, more importantly, in terms of their quality and likelihood of purchasing. This leads to continuous improvement of marketing expenditures on the programs that generate the best leads.

Our profiled companies have applied these Sales 2.0 methods:

☐   WebEx can predict its cost per qualified lead as well as its revenue results, based on a commitment to grading and tracking leads by both marketing and sales.

☐   At Genius.com, marketing supports sales by running programs to engage prospects, draw them to their web site, and elicit their interest in a demo or trial. Conversions from one sales cycle stage to the next are carefully tracked and measured, along with web site visits and cost per click so that marketing can repeat the most successful campaigns.

Imperative 3: Define an Improved Sales Process and Commit to It

While creating an innovative business process is less visible than developing a new product or investing in factories, our research shows it is actually more important to a company's success.

—Dr. Andrew McAfee, Associate Professor at Harvard
Business School, and Dr. Erik Brynjolfsson, Professor of
Management at MIT's Sloan School of Management, "Dog
Eat Dog," *Wall Street Journal,* April 28, 2007

As McAfee and Brynjolfsson's research indicates, introducing process to all areas of your business, including sales, can have more of an impact on your results than other investments. Everybody pays lip service to the importance of sales process, but few companies have really paid attention to designing one that works; even fewer businesses are disciplined about following their process. Sales can be a repeatable, scalable, dependable function, but only if companies insist upon adherence to a customer-centric sales process that focuses on sales-rep efficiency and effectiveness and which is reinforced by sales managers who directly manage reps. The sales process defines each step that a sales rep takes to convert prospects into customers as well as the actions that buyers and sellers must each take in order to progress to the next step. It helps management understand the company's key business metrics and ongoing revenue forecast. It is a strategic framework that not only tracks productivity but also gives everyone a common language to describe and measure productivity, and it is a competitive advantage to understand and continually improve sales-cycle metrics.

Sales 2.0 companies recognize that defining a sales process cannot be done in a vacuum. Your sales process is unique to your customers and must be tailored to their buying processes, business goals, and deadlines. Companies with more than one market or customer type (such as *Fortune* 500 companies and small and medium-size businesses [SMBs]) may have multiple sales processes since these disparate customers often buy in a different manner. Sales reps who understand how a customer buys, how they want to interact with you, what their buying style is, what's important to them personally, how decision making occurs in their company, how they will measure success, or what needs to be in place before they can make a purchase will move the sales cycle forward effectively. The most successful reps will develop long-term relationships with customers and collaborate to ensure that ROI—as measured by the customer—is delivered after a purchase is made and the product is put to use. The sales process should be flexible, too. Forcing customers through a script or rigid step-by-step sales cycle regardless of their situation will not increase productivity. Table 6.1 shows how an aligned customer buying process and sales process for an initial purchase might be put into practice.

The sales process should also be designed to help sales reps sell. Sales 1.0 reps may bristle at the idea of following set processes and systems with customers and worry that it will kill their creativity. They will make assumptions about losing their ability to use intuitive people skills in their chosen profession and may need to be sold on the benefits of a sales process. But good sales reps who are self-disciplined and self-motivated are easily won over when they see evidence that by following a disciplined process—supported by technology that makes it easy to do so—they will increase their individual productivity and make more money. You need to demonstrate, by leadership and example, that by

TABLE 6.1   Aligned Buying and Selling Processes

Buying Process	Selling Process
1. Define problem	1. Define qualified prospect profile
2. Research solutions	2. Generate/attract prospects
3. Engage/prequalify vendors	3. Engage/prequalify prospects
4. Build trust/evaluate vendors	4. Develop relationship
5. Evaluate product	5. Offer trial/evaluation
6. Evaluate proposal	6. Send/negotiate proposal
7. Select/approve	7. Request approvals
8. Purchase	8. Close

implementing a process, you are not trying to impose freedom-inhibiting rules. You are supplying your reps with a tool for self-management and motivation that will help them to be more successful. By piloting a sales process with a small number of Sales 2.0 reps, who are open and naturally drawn to process and automation—and celebrating the associated success very publicly—you will easily win over the other reps who are able to make the culture shift to Sales 2.0. Nothing breeds success faster than success.

And, of course, when your reps participate in creating processes, they are more apt to embrace them. Process creation and fine-tuning can and should include sales rep input and collaboration for continuously improving optimal sales steps and methods of engaging customers. And through another collaborative effort—best-practices sharing—the best sales processes are proliferated through the organization, usually facilitated by management. It also makes good sense to invest in sales-process training followed by on-the-job coaching by sales managers to ensure that sales reps actually follow defined processes. Josiane Feigon, President of TeleSmart Communications—a global sales training company specializing in Inside Sales training—emphasizes the importance of including first-line managers in the training process. They are the ones who make sales process stick by continually reinforcing it in their sales organizations.

The 2008 CSO Insights *Sales Performance Optimization Report* shows a direct correlation between sales-process training and consistent use. Additionally, firms that invest the time and effort to understand their prospects' buy cycles benefit from improved performance, much higher conversion rates from proposal to sale than other survey participants, and a shorter sales cycle.

Imperative 4: Use the Sales Process Strategically

Consider this scenario: It's nearing the last month of the quarter. Your field reps are swamped closing end-of-quarter business. Knowing your metrics, you see in your sales process reports that you don't have enough in the pipeline to keep your reps busy with qualified opportunities in the first month of next quarter. But you know what to do. You work with your marketing department and your Inside Sales group to increase lead generation campaigns to get your pipeline ready with qualified leads.

The reward for designing a sales process and having everyone in sales follow it is the wealth of information you get as a result—including understanding pipeline and forecast metrics. Once your sales process is defined and accepted, it also becomes the yardstick by which you're able to measure and improve sales performance and productivity. It also starts to serve as a business-intelligence hub. As you begin to understand the predictability of the process over time, it will serve as your crystal ball for predicting the future. When you measure and track your sales effectiveness, the science or analytical part of the sales process becomes very powerful—whether you are entering a new market or managing a sales cycle for an existing one. Sales process metrics are especially critical for high-volume markets and for companies testing new markets, products, pricing, customer targets, messaging, positioning, or marketing programs. Customer relationship management (CRM) and related applications such as Business Analytics are typically used to capture and measure sales-process data.

Unfortunately, most sales managers measure the wrong things—or they only measure one thing: revenue. It is true that the sales department is *ultimately* measured on one major metric. But measuring *only* revenue hinders your ability to assess sales performance in the middle of a month or quarter. By the end of the period in question, you've either made or missed the number. Only leading indicators—the movements and changes in your sales process—enable you to make mid-course corrections that can have an impact on your quarterly results, on both an organizational and individual rep level, before the quarter closes. When you understand on a weekly basis what is moving in or out of the pipeline—what is increasing and decreasing at each step in the sales process—you can begin to predict results as well as understand the sales activities and conversions required to generate a certain revenue target. Focusing on revenue alone will not lead to process improvement, as revenue is a trailing indicator.

A measurable sales process also uncovers key data about your business. It can be used to test assumptions associated with go-to-market strategies for new products and customers—as well as new marketing and sales approaches for existing ones. With new products and customers, sales leaders often have unrealistic expectations about sales performance that stem from misperceptions about key metrics such as ASP, conversion rates from step to step in your sales cycle, the number of qualified leads needed to make quota, how much revenue one rep can generate, and how quickly a new rep can reach full productivity. You can use your sales process to test different target audiences, or positioning or pricing strategies. If you are expanding your sales organization, having performance data for your existing sales employees will allow you to accurately target revenue expectations when you hire additional sales reps. A tested and documented sales process helps ramp up new reps more quickly as well. The earlier you can bring them up to speed and contributing revenue, the better for your company and the more motivating for your reps.

Sales-process measurement is also important for continuous improvement in managing sales cycles. Sales 2.0 companies do not define process once, assume standard metrics, and settle. Consistent measurement makes it possible to pinpoint specific areas for improvement and test different marketing and sales approaches. It can also help set realistic goals for the future. Similarly, changes in known metrics may signal market changes—and give you early warning signs of revenue shortfalls that could affect your financials. This is your crystal ball. For example, knowing your qualified lead numbers are trending low for the quarter will give you the flexibility to delay major expenses or hiring decisions into a future quarter and keep profit constant. On the flip side, if your metrics show better results than average, you could accelerate hiring to ensure proper territory coverage for consistent customer responsiveness and avoid leaving money on the table.

In this simplified example, for a company with a six-month sales cycle, the number of leads generated dropped in the second quarter, which resulted in fewer qualified leads reaching the sales pipeline than in the previous quarter. The effects of this decrease would have shown up two quarters later, in the fourth quarter, with a $3 million shortfall. With Sales 2.0 process tracking, the early warning system or crystal ball (see Figure 6.1) alerted the company to signs of trouble two quarters in advance, which allowed them to run additional marketing campaigns and head off a revenue shortfall.

In addition to economic slowdowns, other market factors that can change the sales process include the emergence of a new competitor, product enhancements, and product line expansions. When these occur, you may need to add or subtract sales cycle steps or the activities needed at different steps, or increase or decrease assumed conversion rates. You may also need to update your recruiting profiles, marketing strategies, and organizational structure as your sales process evolves with new or changing market conditions or customer types.

As you roll out and test your Sales 2.0 initiatives, you can track and measure their specific results using your sales process metrics. If you are evaluating Sales 2.0 technology solutions, being aware of your sales cycle steps and areas for improvement will help you determine which ones might have the most impact on your business. Many technologies available today optimize a particular step in the sales process, support increased interaction and engagement with your customer, or enable measurement and analytics of the process itself.

Having a sales process will also help you objectively evaluate and compare individual sales performance. If reps are headed for a bad quarter, you'll be able to diagnose their underperformance in advance of quarter-end by determining whether their activity levels or conversion metrics (or both) are off. The model can help you map the sales process and metrics of your best-performing reps and compare them with the rest of your sales organization. When you detect what makes them different—other than the revenue they deliver at the end of the quarter—you can begin to identify their winning strategies and make these the standard across your group.

Compare your metrics with industry standards or peers outside your company to evaluate your sales effectiveness in the market. Understanding sales-process metrics leads to predictable, reliable sales forecasting, a much sought-after trend for the investment community and senior management alike. It is nice to be optimistic about sales, but being accurate

The Crystal Ball

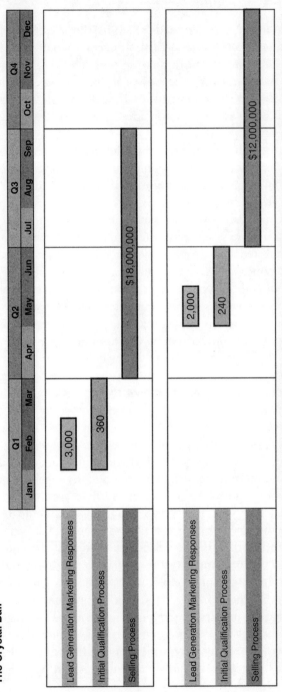

	Q1			Q2			Q3			Q4		
	Jan	Feb	Mar	Apr	May	Jun	Jul	Aug	Sep	Oct	Nov	Dec

Lead Generation Marketing Responses — 3,000
Initial Qualification Process — 360
Selling Process — $18,000,000

Lead Generation Marketing Responses — 2,000
Initial Qualification Process — 240
Selling Process — $12,000,000

Note: If measuring all activities per standard Sales 2.0 practice, any increase or decrease in a marketing program result can be an early warning sign of looming disaster or upside opportunity 2 to 3 quarters in advance.

Figure 6.1 The Sales 2.0 Early Warning System or Crystal Ball

and setting appropriate expectations based on real data is preferable. Shareholders and investors get uncomfortable when actual results don't match forecasted results. They can react negatively and decrease the value of your company.

Here is how some of the companies profiled in Part 3 of this book implement sales process to great advantage:

☐   WebEx's pipeline-management philosophy emphasizes "shape and velocity" measurements rather than volume. WebEx can predict its quarterly results with a high degree of accuracy, due to its advanced use of sales process analysis.

☐   Syneron's Sales 2.0 pilots revealed a more accurate picture of its ASP and sales-process metrics, including contact rates that were better than assumptions. This intelligence allowed the company to make predictable pipeline and revenue assumptions going forward.

Imperative 5: Create Personalized, Long-Term, Collaborative Relationships with Prospects and Customers

Your customers may all be in the banking business, but they couldn't be more different. One company likes to receive quarterly phone calls at a regularly scheduled time to discuss its next quarter's goals and how your product can help meet them. Another prefers ad hoc e-mail and chat communication to get pricing and product availability updates as their business and initiatives change.

Customer relationships have always been important in sales. But Sales 2.0 requires a new way of thinking about and engaging with customers. Successful Sales 2.0 reps help customers buy the way they want to buy. It is now more critical than ever to focus on customers' business results and communications preferences and work toward long-term relationships rather than thinking of customer opportunities as short-term wins at the end of the quarter. Reps who rely on pitching product features and benefits and strong-arming customers to buy because it's the end of the quarter will not gain trust and respect. But Sales 2.0 reps do not resort to such tactics, and even go several steps further with their clients: They learn about customers' personal styles, communications preferences, and future plans. They are rewarded for this buy/sell align-ment with customer loyalty and repeat purchases.

Customers are gravitating to expedient means of communication and information capture: online and by phone. It is now possible to make conversations and meetings highly interactive, personal, and engaging—even if you never meet your customer face-to-face. This is especially important in the early stages of relationships when you are establishing rapport and trust, and the customer is qualifying *you*. It is essential to web-enable your sales and marketing teams to meet this growing need.

Sales 2.0 leaders are focused on creating lasting, collaborative rela-tionships with customers:

☐   Oracle and WebEx both use visual, interactive tools during phone calls with prospects to increase engagement.

☐   All the companies we profile in Part 3 have sales teams dedicated to customers to emphasize the importance of customer relationships and deepen those relationships beyond the initial purchase. As a result, everyone wins: Customers receive better service, and sales reps generate additional revenue. This also allows another team of reps to focus on generating new business, leveraging the company's sales efforts.

Imperative 6: Facilitate Team Selling and Best-Practices Sharing

In Sales 2.0 companies, members of different sales organizations—such as field sales and Inside Sales—work together to engage and serve cus-tomers. They often do this with the help of technical or product spe-cialists, and legal or contracts staff. Organizations, job descriptions, and compensation plans are structured to support this team approach rather than creating channel conflict by having ill-defined roles, responsibili-ties, territories, and compensation plans that pit one salesperson against another to win the same customer.

Here's an example: your field reps share their territory selling re-sponsibilities with two Inside Sales reps. One, a sales development rep, has a qualified lead quota and is responsible for keeping the pipeline full with prospects who are qualified to buy. The other is a telesales rep who has an individual quota for customers who buy by phone and Internet. In your business, territories may be defined by size of company or sales opportunity. You may distinguish between new and existing accounts and assign those territories separately. Or you may leave it up to the sales team to work together and determine who works with whom on a customer-by-customer basis. In addition to commissions for meeting individual sales quotas, everyone on the sales team also receives a territory bonus or commissions for reaching sales targets in a shared territory. Sales 2.0 managers hire sales reps who think of customers as "our customer," a shared company asset, instead of "my customer," and support that way of thinking with appropriate compensation plans.

Best-practices sharing is also imperative for process improvement and collaboration. Unfortunately, two major problems have come in the way of best-practices sharing in the past: lack of defined processes and conflicting sales culture. We've already discussed how tracking and measuring sales-cycle steps and activities within those steps can provide insights to which reps are using the sales approaches worth sharing. In addition to scheduling face-to-face or web team meetings to discuss how to enhance customer experiences and improve sales productivity, Sales 2.0 companies have processes for sharing best practices, supported by technologies such as CRM and managed internal wikis, blogs, and portals. The Oracle profile in Part 3 describes how some of these systems are used to capture and provide access to global team knowledge.

Team meetings are a commonly used venue for sharing best practices. Sales reps often dread meetings; they would rather be talking to customers than sitting around talking about forecasts. But shown in a different light, these online or in-person staff meetings can be opportunities for reps to talk—brag even!—about their processes and successes. Managers who encourage best practices sharing in this context provide opportunities for reps to learn from each other and enjoy the added benefit of giving recognition to the reps whose practices have been identified as most effective. Pairing experienced reps with newer ones in a buddy system is another approach for reps to share best practices—and yes, even experienced reps can learn from newbies. Numerous approaches can work for your organization, but it's important that managers have a process for capturing the best practices, encouraging team members to improve them constantly, and teaching them to new reps as well as experienced ones.

The culture issue, however, may be the more challenging bridge to cross when implementing best-practices sharing. In sales organizations of the past, individual competition has been valued much more than working together as a group toward a common goal. Compensation plans have reinforced that individual-contributor behavior. Think about most compensation-plan bonuses, for example. They typically reward the top rep or territory with extra cash or special prizes in addition to commissions. Why would anyone want to share their successful sales approaches with their teammates or with other sales territories if it could cost them money? While you don't want to stop rewarding your top-performing reps, you would do well to create a more cooperative sales environment—one that is supported by compensation that rewards team-goal achievements and best-practices sharing in addition to individual contribution. There is growing support for collaboration in business:

☐   According to CSO Insights' statistics, using CRM systems to share best practices is contributing to higher win rates, shorter ramp-up times for new reps, lower sales-rep turnover, and other positive metrics.

☐   In Silicon Valley, there are business organizations that meet and communicate online to share industry best practices in sales, including the Telebusiness Alliance for Inside Sales managers and the Sales Operations Forum for sales effectiveness professionals (*www.sales20book.com/resources*).

Imperative 7: Revisit Sales Employee Profile

We see it in company after company: experienced sales reps—who have been successful for 20 years selling the same Sales 1.0 way—are now having trouble engaging with customers. They used to be able to reach their customers on the phone; now all they get is voicemail. They are being asked to make their sales presentations over the Web, but they've never given a seminar online. These reps used to own their territory and call all the shots with customers; now they have to share their ground with an Inside Sales rep, and they're not happy about that.

In order to achieve superior results, Sales 2.0 requires a culture shift. Your sales reps have to be open to change. They must be willing to interact with colleagues and customers in an open, trusting, collaborative, and authentic way, often at a distance. They may share their sales territory with other sales reps. They may have a team-selling quota.

It's equally important—in order for reps to sell in the way the customer is buying—to learn to communicate using new technologies that their prospects and customers are implementing. In the future, more and more selling activities will be done by telephone and Internet rather than by face-to-face interactions. This new way of selling may not be natural for many experienced sales reps. You can address the transition with training for Sales 1.0 reps and a revised Sales 2.0 hiring profile and interview process for new hires in sales. For example, Genius.com and WebEx interviews include phone calls and online demos to determine if candidates possess Sales 2.0 skills, given the importance of mastering selling using online technology in their environments.

In the coming decade, Sales 2.0 will be a great fit for young sales reps of the future; the open, hip, and happening youth culture is naturally inclined to technology and collaboration. They think more about we than about me: for example, Oracle Sales has changed its culture considerably in the last 20 years. It the 1980s, field reps that weren't used to sharing their territories were asked to do so with a newly founded Inside Sales group. Team incentives were limited in favor of aggressive individual quotas, which created internal competition and channel conflict. Today's field reps have shifted their mindset, after over two decades of coexisting with the highly professional and productive OracleDirect organization. In addition to individual quotas, field and inside reps carry team quotas and work collaboratively to serve their customers.

Imperative 8: Implement Technology to Improve Results

Sales reps and managers now have a cornucopia of software and services available for measuring and optimizing the sales process, increasing forecast predictability, and engaging and collaborating in new ways with customers and colleagues. The technology choices that promise to make it easier for customers to buy and sales managers to automate or improve sales productivity can be overwhelming. So—rather than introducing new technology into your organization because it's cool—choose products that can address a specific area for improvement. Defining and measuring your sales process first and understanding your problem areas will provide indicators for which technologies may be most effective in improving results. Still, it is important to perhaps select one technology at a time, so as not to confuse your reps—or customers—with too many new things at once; then provide training, and give new systems time to have an impact on your group's productivity.

In the open, sharing, and experimental culture of Sales 2.0, sales reps may discover sales tools that help them sell by searching online or comparing notes with friends in sales roles inside or outside your company. They may have favorite communication technologies that they use in their personal lives, and discover ways to employ them effectively in the workplace. Sales reps who find and recommend technology to their peers and management have ultimate credibility when they report their successes to their groups. Sales 2.0 companies welcome these grassroots recommendations, which could very well lead to better user adoption and improved results than management mandates to use technology.

As we suggested with other Sales 2.0 initiatives, pilot new technology with a small group for several quarters; determine what reps like about it, and what they struggle with; measure its impact on sales results by taking before and after measurements of your sales process; and work out the kinks and make changes before rolling it out to larger groups or your whole organization.

In Part 4, we discuss getting started with Sales 2.0 technologies and show how some companies are realizing measurable gains in productivity with their use.

7
R U SALES 2.0? A CHECKLIST

Now that you've been introduced to the key concepts of Sales 2.0, use this checklist to see how your organization rates. But don't get discouraged if you don't meet all the criteria. U R Sales 2.0 if your organization is even questioning and starting to experiment with improving sales efficiency, effectiveness and business results using innovative sales practices and technology.

Strategy

☐   Aligned product, marketing, and sales strategies consistent with your target customer markets supported by your CEO, department head, and rest of the company.

☐   Sales team organized strategically with most appropriate and cost-effective sales channels possible used to reach new and current customers.

☐   Lower-cost communications media (i.e., the telephone, the Internet) used in all sales channels; traveling only when expense is justified.

☐   Appropriate investments in marketing to generate the quality and volume of sales leads necessary to achieve your revenue numbers.

☐   New strategic initiatives piloted first (even in start-ups).

People

☐   Process-oriented, open, flexible, customer-focused, tech-savvy team players that can be successful given your Sales 2.0 strategy and the job required.

☐   Sales reps focused on creating lasting customer relationships that are collaborative and authentic.

☐   Collaborative relationship between sales and marketing as well as among different selling groups. Team selling is facilitated and supported by organization structure, training, and compensation.

☐   Sales collaboration with other departments such as product development, information technology (IT), product or support groups, finance, and contracts to advocate for the customer and streamline the sales process.

☐   Sales managers committed to process and metrics management, and to figuring out how to make it work for their reps and customers.

☐   Processes exist for best-practices sharing, enforced with training, coaching, and technology.

Process

☐   Measurable, predictable sales process, designed around your target customer's measurable business requirements, buying or decision-making process, and personal buying style.

☐   Defined and documented lead ranking system, agreement on what constitutes a qualified lead, and number needed to reach quota agreed upon by sales and marketing.

☐   Knowledge and tracking of key metrics, including conversion rates from step to step, average selling price (ASP), average sales cycle, and ramp-up time for new employees.

☐   Sales process reexamined, fine-tuned, continuously improved, and used to predict business trends and results.

☐ Sales process integrated with other processes involving your customer, including order fulfillment, billing, service or support, and account management.

Technology

☐ Systems and tools appropriately mapped to your sales process and helping customers buy to enhance sales performance rather than make it more difficult.

☐ Web site and online tools engage customers and provide self-service opportunities to learn about your company and products.

☐ Technology automates tracking, measurement and reporting on key metrics, which are used to improve your sales process and individual rep and group performance.

☐ Technology addresses needs you have identified by understanding your customers' communications and buying preferences, your sales process, relationships and engagement levels, and how they can be improved.

☐ Technology is tested and implemented incrementally to increase user adoption and enable you to measure its impact on your sales effectiveness.

PART 2

Your Entry into Sales 2.0

INSIDE SALES—THE STRATEGIC CENTRAL NERVOUS SYSTEM OF SALES 2.0

One of the most effective ways to begin the strategic journey to Sales 2.0 is to design and implement professional Inside Sales functions—either sales development for lead qualification or telesales for revenue generation, or both. These sales functions are no longer tactical nice-to-haves; they can play a critical role in your company's evolution to Sales 2.0 because they embody all the key principles of Sales 2.0: they can leverage or potentially replace traditional field sales organizations; they are fundamentally metrics, process, and technology-driven; and they use innovative, online ways to engage and develop relationships with prospects. Most customers are as concerned about their efficiency and productivity in the buying process as we salespeople are about our sales process. No wonder we are doing more business by phone and the Web than ever before.

Inside Sales is strategic to a Sales 2.0 organization because:

☐ It optimizes the alignment of sales resources to the opportunity types each sales channel can best service.

☐ It enables better, more immediate communication and more interactions with customers and the market in general.

☐ It is a source of customer and prospect information, which when tapped properly by the rest of the company is critical for sales, marketing, and product development purposes.

☐ Sales development teams increase revenue by improving customer engagement early in the sales cycle as well as field and telesales productivity and effectiveness later in the sales cycle.

☐ Telesales teams provide a more efficient and profitable way for customers to buy, thereby closing more sales and capturing otherwise missed market opportunities.

☐ Telesales addresses customers who are not being contacted by field resources such as small and medium-size sales opportunities and follow-on business.

☐ Inside Sales metrics provide the crystal-ball opportunity to peer into the future to improve forecast accuracy and drive repeatable success.

The number of sales leaders who still believe (incorrectly!) that the Inside Sales function is relatively inconsequential and comprising solely junior salespeople is decreasing. More and more businesses recognize the strategic importance that the Inside Sales organization can have on creating opportunities, closing revenue, and providing ongoing service to customers while providing critical insights into businesses that lead to forecast predictability. Using Sales 2.0 practices, the Inside Sales function is having a positive impact on customer experience, sales productivity, and business results.

The successful implementation of Inside Sales can drive the rest of your sales channels to Sales 2.0 by demonstrating the results and predictability associated with these innovative sales practices. The amount of selling that happens from the inside—as opposed to traditional face-to-face selling—is increasing exponentially around the world, and especially in Silicon Valley, where many business-changing innovations are born. Why is this happening? In Part 1, we showed that many companies have an imperative to change the way they sell due to many factors, such as customers' changing communications preferences, shifting power from sales reps to customers, and rising sales costs. Sales groups using Sales 2.0 processes, many of which are enabled by new technologies, are producing more sales at a lower cost and with greater predictability—and they are doing more of it without travel. Therefore, optimizing the overall sales organization's productivity involves placing a greater emphasis on Inside Sales.

This is not to say that field sales visits are not critically important for some companies and customers; in certain situations a customer requires a face-to-face meeting in order to make a purchasing decision. Unfortunately, far too many companies send out costly field sales resources when it's not a requirement for the prospect or when the expense of a visit isn't justified by the qualification level or potential lifetime value of that customer. Many companies could do a better job considering what the customer really needs as well as the profitability associated with the customer and the sales opportunity at hand. They need to think about how the customer prefers to buy and the cost of attaining a customer relative to the value of that customer's initial and ongoing purchases. As a result, even traditional field salespeople are performing more of their work using Sales 2.0 best practices that were piloted and developed by the Inside Sales organization.

With complex sales cycles, there are steps that are more efficiently *and* more effectively handled by inside resources. For example, field salespeople who excel at negotiation and closing are often not equally proficient at generating and qualifying volumes of leads, which does a disservice to prospects in the early stages of the sales cycle. The professional skills of a field salesperson are typically better used in the later stages of a sales cycle than at the beginning. A sales channel strategy that includes Inside Sales allows companies to strategically align their sales resources to the appropriate customer opportunities, better serve customers not visited by field salespeople, affordably capture market share in smaller accounts, and profitably sell deals with a smaller average selling price (ASP).

The process and transactional volume benefits associated with a professional Inside Sales organization are intuitively clear. But we've learned that in addition to a disciplined sales process, customer relationship-building is also important for improving sales performance. Many sales managers worry about the level of customer engagement and sales possible without meeting prospects face-to-face. With technology such as web meetings or web collaboration, web cams, social networking, e-mail, and web response tracking, Inside Sales reps can personalize interactions, and build and sustain strong customer relationships. They can make their sales calls *visual and interactive* even though the customer is in a remote location. Today's Sales 2.0 technologies enable improvements to processes *and* customer relationships.

8
WHAT IS INSIDE SALES?

Inside Sales organizations communicate with customers using the telephone and online tools such as e-mail, the Web, and other Internet-based technologies. Inside Sales includes sales development—a group that generates qualified sales leads—and telesales—a group that generates revenue.

Part of the confusion surrounding the Inside Sales function is that there are few naming standards. The terms we've heard include telesales, web-touch sales, Internet sales, headquarters sales, corporate sales, direct sales, lead qualification, and business development. A very old term for these groups is telemarketing, but professional business-to-business Inside Sales operations almost never use this term because it brings to mind low-level script readers who call you at home when you least want to be interrupted. That is not at all what Inside Sales 2.0 is about.

Within Inside Sales organizations, there is typically a distinction made between two kinds of groups, sometimes reporting to one sales manager. There are those who close sales just as field salespeople do, but who do so without face-to-face interactions. And there are those who engage with prospects in the earliest stages of a sales cycle to help them start their buying process, determine how qualified they are to buy, and deliver these qualified leads to a quota-carrying salesperson, either in the field or telesales. In this book, we refer to the first group—the revenue-generating group—as telesales, and the second—or the lead-generation and qualification group—as sales development. Inside Sales includes sales development and telesales.

SALES DEVELOPMENT AND TELESALES: WHICH IS RIGHT FOR YOUR COMPANY?

The use of Inside Sales and the structure that makes sense for you depend on your business, products, market, customers, competitors, and even company culture. As we look at the roles of sales development and telesales, keep in might that Sales 2.0 companies:

☐   Align the right sales resources with the right opportunity types at the right time to maximize customer acquisition and profitability.
☐   Follow technology-enabled sales processes that help customers buy in the way they want to buy.
☐   Experiment with new ways to engage customers and improve sales productivity.

When you think about restructuring your sales organization to include Inside Sales functions, think about sports. A football team, for example, does not have 11 quarterbacks on the field. It has a mix of positions, each with different roles and responsibilities, all coordinated to achieve the best results with the least risk. Similarly, a Sales 2.0 organization is not made up exclusively of quota-carrying field salespeople, but a mix of complementary functions and resources.

Inside Sales can round out your sales team and make it more productive while improving service to a wider range of customers. All forms of Inside Sales involve communicating with the customer and furthering the buying and sales cycles—whether the measurable end result for you is a qualified lead, an appointment, an event registration, or a sale—and they do so without traveling. Sales development and telesales groups have the same objectives: understanding the prospect's business needs, how your company's products meets those needs, and moving prospective clients either toward becoming a customer or out of the sales funnel.

Here are some of the typical ways Sales 2.0 companies employ telesales and sales development groups within their Inside Sales organization:

Sales Development

☐ Generate, qualify, nurture, manage, and deliver sales leads to telesales or field sales.
☐ Make appointments for field salespeople or channel partners.
☐ Enroll prospects in events, such as conferences or seminars.
☐ Usually partner with one or more telesales or field salespeople.

Telesales

☐ Sell new business into a territory, based on geography, size or type of account, vertical industry, product line, order size, or some other basis (e.g., customers with under $100M in annual revenue, named accounts, resellers, or partners); sometimes referred to as "hunting."
☐ Sell upgrades and add-on business to customers while strengthening relationships; sometimes referred to as "farming."
☐ Sell subscriptions, renewals, maintenance, or service agreements.
☐ Work individually or as a team with other members of the sales organization.

9

SALES DEVELOPMENT: GENERATING, QUALIFYING, AND MANAGING LEADS

I magine what it might be like to be this prospective customer: weeks ago, you requested a report by filling out a form on a company web site. Since nothing has been delivered and you need the information for a meeting with your manager tomorrow, you've called the company three times. But you still haven't heard from them. You're thinking that it's probably time to check out the competition.

Is it possible that this is happening to *your* prospects?

Quota-carrying salespeople, whether they are inside or field reps, get busy. When they have plenty of prospects who are close to buying, they may ignore potential customers who are just starting their buying cycle. Field salespeople are on the road a lot. And they are usually better at engaging prospective customers when they are closer to making a purchase decision.

Another recurring theme we hear a lot, especially from underperforming sales reps, is "I don't have enough leads." Organizations that assign the responsibility of lead generation to quota-carrying salespeople usually end up with a shortage of sales leads, given that salespeople often view these activities as undesirable tasks to be avoided. A core Sales 2.0 strategy involves building your sales organization with sales experts dedicated to the pipeline-building stage of the sales process, which ensures that new prospects are constantly being developed and nurtured. When buyers are engaged with you, they are less likely to get lost.

Implementing a sales development team that communicates with and manages prospect relationships in the early stages of the sales cycle is one of the most effective ways to ensure a steady and predictable delivery to the field or telesales of qualified leads who are ready to buy. The sales development group is dedicated to a prospective customer's experience early in your company's relationship with them. They don't travel, so they are virtually always available by phone and Web. Sales development also leverages your more expensive and highly skilled sales resources. Because prospects have access to this dedicated resource, sales reps can focus more time on closing sales—either by phone and Web, or face-to-face. And by measuring the development and outcome of this continual pipeline of sales opportunities through the sales process, your quarterly revenue will become more consistent and predictable.

Also, by removing unqualified opportunities from the pipeline early in the sales cycle, sales development determines which accounts will be followed up by the salesforce and thereby paves the way for increased close rates by the field and telesales. By compensating sales development reps (SDRs) on generating qualified leads or appointments, you can avoid running the pipeline dry every quarter and having your salesforce scramble to find new opportunities. SDRs enable salespeople to focus on selling to qualified accounts and closing deals without forfeiting long-term pipeline development.

Sales development reps are often organized by territories that align with other sales organizations, such as the field, channels, and telesales. One sales development rep typically supports three to five quota-carrying salespeople, and in larger companies that ratio may be closer to one to one.

SALES DEVELOPMENT RETURN ON INVESTMENT

In any organization, investments in new sales groups have to be justified. The example below illustrates the financial impact of adding a small sales development team to a field sales organization of 16 reps. In our example, four SDRs were hired, each supporting four reps in the field. At the end of the first year, each field salesperson closed one more order per quarter, or four more per year, because he or she had sales development reps helping prospects and identifying qualified leads. This allowed the field to focus more time working with qualified opportunities; four more customers were able to buy!

The ROI of sales development is compelling as well (Table 9.1). In this example, the annual sales staffing costs are $180,000 per field salesperson, $75,000 per sales development rep, $150,000 for a sales development manager, plus a 35 percent "benefit load" for each, and the average selling price (ASP) is $100,000. After implementing sales development, this company produced $6.4 million in additional revenue, 25 percent more than with field sales alone, for an added cost of $607,500, resulting in a revenue return on investment of 1,053 percent.

One of the most rewarding ways to move your Sales 1.0 organization toward Sales 2.0 is to implement a sales development team. You can start small with one or two people, test your process, and refine it

TABLE 9.1   Return on Investment of Sales Development

	Field Sales Only Model	Field Sales + Sales Development
Number of field salespeople	16	16
Number of sales development reps	0	4
Number of transactions each field rep closes per year	16	20
Average selling price	$100,000	$100,000
Resulting field team revenue per year	$25.6 million	$32 million
Sales resources cost	$3,888,000	$4,495,500
Incremental revenue sourced from sales development team	$0	$6.4 million
Incremental revenue returned on investment	0%	1,053%

before hiring more staff and making further investments. The Syneron profile in Part 3 includes a good illustration of piloting sales development. Later in this chapter, we include another example of a sales development pilot that created a whole new department at salesforce.com.

SALES LEAD RANKING

The sales development function makes a major contribution to process measurement, one of the foundations of Sales 2.0. Sales development reps provide valuable information to marketing on which programs are most effective and profitable. By determining a customer's readiness to buy and scoring prospects according to their likelihood of becoming a purchasing customer, they help marketing evaluate different programs by capturing data on customer responses and identifying the events or programs that produce the best outcome in terms of lead volume and quality. By tracking these leads through the sales cycle, you can determine which marketing expenditures produce the most customers and also evaluate sales development's effect on the pipeline and revenue.

Prospects who engage online are often asked to enter information about themselves and their businesses, which can be used to automatically assign a lead ranking. Those interacting live with SDRs are ranked based on their responses to qualification questions that are part of the Sales 2.0 sales process. Lead scoring allows quota-carrying reps to prioritize and focus their time on the prospects who are most qualified and likely to make a purchase.

When designing your lead ranking system, follow the Sales 2.0 practice of collaborating with marketing so everybody is on the same page. If you are just getting started with a sales lead ranking process, you'll need to test it and prepare to make adjustments. Customer and market changes may also necessitate updates to your sales lead ranking definitions, as well as your sales process. As with other Sales 2.0 initiatives, start with a small group and then roll out to your entire sales organization when you've fine-tuned the definitions.

Table 9.2 is an example of sales lead ranking or scoring criteria.

TABLE 9.2 Lead Ranking System

Rank	Definition	Description	Action
A	Excellent business potential	Meets qualified lead criteria (identifiable business problem/pain that fits your scope) Actively looking to solve problem Has interest in buying a solution within 6 months Contact has functional responsibility Is willing to talk to/meet with a sales rep Budget exists for solution	Pass lead to sales—set appointment
B	Good business potential	Meets qualified lead criteria (identifiable business problem/pain that fits your scope) Has interest in buying a solution within 6–12 months Contact has functional responsibility and/or is a decision maker Is willing to talk to/meet with a sales rep Possible budget exists, or could be developed	Pass lead to sales—set appointment
C	Business potential not defined	Info gathering, thinks there is a problem Fits your prospect profile More development required Sponsor has been or will be identified	Sales development rep cultivates until upgraded to A/B lead Continue marketing and call back in 3 months
D	Latent potential	Tire-kicker/little interest May be willing to do something at some point in the future Five attempts/no response	Rank and leave in database for future marketing campaigns
X	No business potential	Not a fit for your solution	Discontinue marketing activities
Y	Bad data	Bounce back from a campaign or purchased list	Delete from database

MEASURING THE BEGINNING OF THE SALES PROCESS: PIPELINE DEVELOPMENT

With your sales lead ranking system in place, you'll be able to use it to achieve Sales 2.0 science in your sales process measurement. You will be tracking customers' progressions from one step of the sales process to the next—or conversions—as they get closer to a buying decision. Sales development uses the sales lead ranking system to separate qualified from unqualified sales opportunities and set priorities for other members of the sales team. In other words, sales development builds the sales pipeline.

The example in Table 9.3 shows the results of a Sales 2.0 sales process and sales development pilot in a start-up company. This company tracked every step of its customers' buying process and established some common metrics. They found that sales development reps were able to make 50 attempts to engage with customers (by phone and e-mail) per day. Of those 50 phone calls and e-mails, they made contact with an average of six prospects (12 percent). Of those six, another 12 percent were identified as "qualified" according to their lead ranking system. Given their ASP of $100,000, the sales process metrics show that one sales development rep can generate a pipeline of $1.58 million in qualified (defined as A&B) opportunities per month.

TABLE 9.3 Sales Process Measurement: Pipeline Development per Sales Development Rep

Metrics	Output Assumption
Number of outbound calls and customer-specific e-mails per day/week/month	50/250/1100
Contacts (connects, returned calls, and returned e-mails) per day/week/month at 12% connection rate	6/30/132
Percent of contacts in A/B lead category	12%
Average number of contacts per month in A/B lead category	15.8
Average sales price	$100,000
Pipeline value per month (A/B leads converted to "evaluating needs" stage opportunity)	$1.58 million

When you first get started with sales development—or any sales position for that matter—you will have new reps who will have a ramp-up period before reaching full productivity. By tracking sales metrics for new hires, the start-up company in our example identified a ramp-up period of three months to reach the results shown in this model. In month one new reps were at 25 percent effectiveness, and at month two, 50 percent. Knowing these values and building them into your model is essential in order to set realistic expectations.

MEASURING THE END OF THE SALES PROCESS: PIPELINE TO REVENUE PROJECTION

Looking further ahead in the sales process, our example company tracked its conversions after prospects were initially qualified and added to the pipeline (Table 9.4). In this case, 50 percent of leads generated by sales development progressed to later stages in the buying cycle, and of those 50 percent, 20 percent became customers. Again, applying the known ASP of $100,000, we can see the projected monthly and annual revenue that can be produced as a result of hiring one sales development rep.

How might this work in your business? You may not know your sales process metrics such as conversion rates, ASP, or even how many prospects are available to contact. The sales process establishes the framework to capture these average values, which gives you critical information and the predictability of a Sales 2.0 company. You'll also start to identify the differences in sales processes between your best

TABLE 9.4 Pipeline to Revenue Projections

Metrics	Output Assumption
Number of A/B leads that will result in next steps in sales cycle (50%)	7.9
Number of opportunities that will close monthly (20%) per sales rep	1.5
Average sales price	$100,000
Projected monthly revenue	$150,000
Projected annual revenue resulting from leads generated by each sales development rep	$1.8 million

performers and more average ones and then share the best practices of the top sellers. You'll determine the places in the sales cycle where improvements could make a real difference to your revenue results. When you see values trending down early in the process, you'll know that you need to make corrections to avoid missing your revenue number. Then you can test the effects of new technology, sales training, different compensation, lead generation, or other programs, using your sales process to measure results.

We encourage you to input and track your own sales process metrics by downloading a free copy of the sales process worksheet from our web site, *www.sales20book.com/resources*. Since every business has different values for each key metric and conversion rate, you'll need to customize it. Then tell us how it works for you!

SPECIALIZED ROLES IN SALES DEVELOPMENT

Sales 2.0 companies recognize that customers respond to sales reps with different kinds of skills at different times in the sales cycle. Sales development reps excel at engaging customers in the early parts of the sales process and leverage other sales team members, who help buyers in the later stages. But even within sales development, further specialization and distinct roles can lead to better customer engagement and more productive use of resources.

There are two distinct kinds of sales development functions:

1. Sales development that qualifies and follows up on incoming leads that engage with the company through the web site or phone, usually driven by marketing programs, and route qualified opportunities to the appropriate quota-carrying salesperson; sometimes called inbound sales development, direct response, or lead qualification.
2. Sales development that initiates calls and e-mails to companies who aren't engaging with you, to source new, incremental sales opportunities and pass them to quota-carrying salespeople; sometimes called outbound sales development, lead generation, prospecting, or cold calling.

In companies where the incoming lead volume justifies having a dedicated inbound sales development function, having separate groups makes your reps more focused and productive. An inbound team only responds to incoming leads generated by marketing programs and follows up on those customer inquiries, and a separate outbound team only prospects for incremental leads. Aaron Ross, founding director of salesforce.com's outbound prospecting group, tells us, "It's very challenging for a rep to switch between the two roles and mindsets throughout the day."

"Salesforce.com learned this the hard way in 2004, when the company changed from having separate sales development teams doing inbound and outbound roles to having the same team handle both inbound and outbound responsibilities. Within a week, productivity in terms of leads generated had dropped by 30 percent. Within three weeks, by tracking the sales process, it was clear that the productivity drop was caused by the mixing of the responsibilities and was not going to improve with time. Salesforce.com quickly changed the structure back to separate teams for the inbound and outbound functions, and productivity rose back to prior levels."

COLD CALLING 2.0

Ideally, your lead generation marketing campaigns generate a steady volume of high-quality Web and phone inquiries from prospective customers. But if they aren't producing enough leads or leads in key accounts that you are targeting, you may have to resort to outbound sales development, or cold calling. Most sales reps, however, detest cold calls, and your customers probably hate them more. They are usually an inefficient and expensive waste of time for both parties. By applying Sales 2.0 practices to this loathsome but sometimes necessary sales activity, you can realize some breakthrough results.

Aaron Ross calls this improved approach to outbound prospecting "Cold Calling 2.0," which he developed and initiated at salesforce.com with resounding success. If Cold Calling 1.0 is the old style of prospecting—calling someone who doesn't know you and who isn't expecting your call—Cold Calling 2.0 uses more effective Sales 2.0 practices. Aaron explains, "Executed systematically, a sales development team devoted exclusively to Cold Calling 2.0 can become the most predictable source of pipeline (and thus revenue) for the company by following a measurable sales process and developing personal relationships with target customers."

Three key principles to developing a Cold Calling 2.0 team are as follows:

1. *No traditional cold calling takes place.* Instead, aim to develop an authentic rapport with customers. Prospect into new accounts without using old tricks and sales techniques such as surprising people on the phone, trying to negotiate around gatekeepers, and sending out generic e-mails. Think like a Sales 2.0 company and consider what a potential customer might respond to. Use online account research tools to learn something about your prospects and their businesses. Find people you know in common using social networking technology, and craft simple, personalized e-mails to generate targeted messages and referrals to the right people, who then expect (and often welcome) a call. With Sales 2.0 technology, you can now track responses to e-mail messages and also determine which pages of your web site your prospect views, which you can use to further customize your follow-ups.

2. *Focus is on results, not activities.* Calls and e-mails per day are much less interesting than the results they produce. Rather, track and compensate reps on metrics such as qualification calls per week, qualified opportunities per month, or closed revenue sourced by the sales development team. Calls-per-day measurements are easily manipulated and can encourage the wrong behaviors, such as reps ending potentially good qualification calls too early so they can move on to making another call. Reps won't be able to meet their qualified lead targets anyway if their activity levels are too low. Knowing your sales process conversion rates will help reps determine how many outreaches are required to make their numbers.

3. *Everything is systematically process-driven, including management practices, hiring, training, and, of course, the actual prospecting process.* This is the essence of a Sales 2.0 practice. By emphasizing repeatability and consistency, the pipeline and revenue ramps generated by a new sales development rep become very predictable, and the entire team's results become highly scalable and repeatable. In addition, marketing investments can be tracked and their ROI calculated. Sales 2.0 technologies, including CRM systems and Sales 2.0 applications, make it easier than ever to take the guesswork out of implementing, executing, and auditing the ROI of prospecting activities.

Aaron concludes, "Cold Calling 2.0 creates a sustainable pipeline engine which drives company revenue. Through 2008, the Cold Calling 2.0 team at salesforce.com will have sourced about $100 million in recurring annual revenue for salesforce.com. Year after year, return on investment on each person in the role is about 3,000 percent, as measured by the revenue produced from the leads they sourced, divided by their loaded annual salary."

SALESFORCE.COM: USING COLD CALLING 2.0 TO REACH MAJOR ACCOUNTS

After launching with a phone and web-based sales organization in 2002, salesforce.com began building a field sales organization dedicated to larger companies. To supplement the inbound leads they received (generated mostly through word of mouth), the field salesforce was expected to prospect to bring in their own large deals. However, little was happening in the way of prospecting. The company realized that the field salespeople were not making many calls because of their understandable dislike for cold calling. Two other factors were becoming apparent:

1. The environment had changed, and the Sales 1.0 prospecting techniques of the 1990s weren't working. Not only were cold calls ineffective, but even targeted marketing programs offering high-value items to large companies produced disappointing results.
2. Field reps making cold calls meant having the highest-cost salespeople performing sales activities that could more efficiently and effectively be handled by other sales resources.

Through these realizations, salesforce.com decided it needed a new approach to create its own controllable, predictable source of a new pipeline. What better place to create a new system than in the middle of a leading CRM company?

At salesforce.com, which used its own CRM system to enable the company's Sales 2.0 best practices, the Cold Calling 2.0 project was begun in 2003 by sales leaders Aaron Ross, Frank Van Veenendaal, and

Shelly Davenport. They spent a year testing and perfecting the practices and system to prove that incremental revenue could be generated
at a high ROI before heavily investing in building a team. In the first
year, two sales development reps, at a loaded cost of about $200,000
combined, sourced leads that resulted in $2 million in revenue. A key
advantage they had was the salesforce.com application itself as a platform on which to track and measure the results of the Cold Calling 2.0
program. Aaron confirms, "We would never have produced the same
level of results without salesforce.com. The Sales 1.0 CRM systems
would have held us back as slow, unintuitive, and lacking the capabilities we needed for things like third-party applications, reporting, and
dashboards."

Despite some serious obstacles, which are detailed below, positive
exponential sales results quickly followed, after the initial period of
fine-tuning (Figure 9.1).

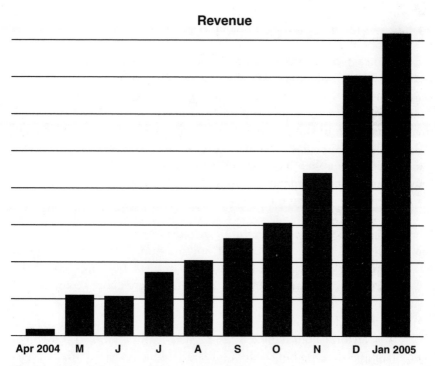

Figure 9.1 Salesforce.com Exponential Growth

Initial Challenges

Aaron reports, "One might assume that the prospecting was easy and that companies would take our calls just because salesforce.com was calling. Nothing could be further from the truth." Although today salesforce.com is a well-known, market-leading CRM vendor with a globally recognized brand, back in the early and mid-2000s, salesforce.com was unknown and misunderstood in most companies. If someone had heard of salesforce.com, he or she typically assumed the company provided outsourced sales teams. Salesforce.com was pioneering the concept of Software-As-A-Service (SaaS), offering its products online and on-demand, but mainstream companies had not yet accepted SaaS.

Furthermore, classic, impersonal prospecting techniques just didn't work anymore. Aaron says, "I decided to throw out all the books and legacy ideas and start from scratch. I also believe that because I had zero sales experience prior to salesforce.com, I had a fresh perspective."

Making the Transition from 1.0 to 2.0

Given the culture shift required in Sales 2.0 thinking, preconceived Sales 1.0 notions about how things should be done can get in the way of innovation. Even in a pioneering company like salesforce.com, Aaron had an advantage over the traditional, newly hired field reps who struggled to make inroads into new, large accounts. His Cold Calling 2.0 vision and execution transformed the way the company did business. Table 9.5 is a summary of how salesforce.com changed its mindset to make the transition from Cold Calling 1.0 to Cold Calling 2.0.

The Sales 2.0 best practices developed at salesforce.com by the sales development team are respectful of the customer; focused on sales rep productivity; are tracked, measured, and fine-tuned; and are dependent on technology. Along with following sales process, here are some of the Cold Calling 2.0 approaches that led to salesforce.com's exponential success:

☐   *Qualify accounts and contacts before calling.* Cold Calling 1.0 involves calling or e-mailing into unfiltered industry-based lists of targets. Prospecting into accounts of marginal potential is the most

TABLE 9.5   Cold Calling 1.0 versus 2.0: What's Changed?

1.0	2.0
Field sales = 90% of prospecting	Sales development = 90% of prospecting
ABC/Always Be Closing	Is there a mutual fit?
Calls per day, appointments	Qualified opportunities/month
Cold calls	Research, referrals
Cheesy sales tricks work	Authenticity works
"I hate this job."	"I learned a lifetime skill."
Long letters and e-mails	Short and sweet text e-mails
CRM hurts productivity	CRM multiplies productivity

common waste of time by sales development reps and their prospects. Spend time collaborating with marketing to identify and clarify your ideal customer profile. Define which companies are the most similar to the top 5 to 10 percent of your customers, defined as the ones likeliest to purchase for the most revenue, and develop target lists based on these criteria.

☐ *Research rather than sell.* Research the customers' business initiatives and find out what they need to buy. Reps make research calls rather than sales calls. The intention is different—instead of trying to access the decision maker on the first call or e-mail, gather information first. Learn about the company and whether there is even a potential fit or not.

☐ *Write BlackBerry-sized e-mails.* Avoid sending long, salesy e-mails that virtually no prospect will take the time to read. Send e-mails that can be read on the screen of a BlackBerry or other mobile e-mail device. Be direct and to the point, and be clear about your message.

☐ *Hire Sales 2.0 professionals and develop their skills.* The sales development role is often treated within a sales organization as a low-level job. If you treat it that way, you'll get low-level results. It's a challenging and often thankless role, but if you treat the team as professionals and recognize them for the value they create, positive results will follow. Don't skimp on training, equipment, or career path development, and set high expectations for continuous improvement.

☐ *Focus on process.* First, understand the customers' needs and buying process, and adjust your sales process and strategy accordingly. Focus also on your internal processes and test and measure several sales ideas or approaches. It's okay and often necessary to have some failures on the road to success. Testing allows you to minimize the time and cost associated with those learning experiences.

☐ *Test new technology.* Enable your sales process with your CRM system and Sales 2.0 applications in every way possible to improve productivity, measurement, and customer engagement. Do you use dashboards? What about applications for de-duplication and data cleansing, contact acquisition, or tools that identify when your prospects visit your web site? There is a wealth of options now to enhance every step of your process; in fact, there are so many options it can be too confusing! Don't let that stop you from constantly testing new applications to see what works for your company.

Can Cold Calling 2.0 Work for Your Company?

The success of the Cold Calling 2.0 project at salesforce.com was a direct result of a well-planned and executed Sales 2.0 program, combining changes in strategy, process, people, and technology. As Aaron pointed out, salesforce.com was a young, relatively unknown company at the time it implemented Cold Calling 2.0, and the company spent many months piloting and testing the results before it ramped up a full team. But its sales leaders were forward-thinking about using innovative sales practices and technology to differentiate its offering and gain market share. Cold Calling 2.0 and other Sales 2.0 approaches certainly helped catapult salesforce.com to a global leadership position.

By following Sales 2.0 practices, other companies have seen similar successes. One of them is Responsys, a leading global provider of on-demand marketing solutions that empowers businesses to market more effectively through e-mail, direct mail, and mobile channels. In late 2007, the company began building a Cold Calling 2.0 program based on the salesforce.com process. Within four months, the team increased its productivity in leads generated per sales development person by 300 percent, and had become the number-one source of pipeline generation in the company.

Cold Calling 2.0 can work for you, too. It is especially effective as an outreach program to new contacts within major or named accounts and is typically profitable for products with an ASP of at least $10,000. The only way you'll know for sure, though, is by testing it. Syneron (one of the companies profiled in Part 3) launched a 12-week pilot program with one experienced rep to test sales process assumptions and fine-tune these expectations before staffing up its sales development team. A pilot is the best way to determine whether Cold Calling 2.0—or any Sales 2.0 initiative—will produce results for you.

10

TELESALES: SELLING BY TELEPHONE AND WEB

Just as sales development provides dedicated attention to early sales cycle customers, telesales ensures sales coverage for qualified customers who because of their company size, initial order size, distance, or other factors might not get attention from other field-based salespeople. Telesales is also the sales channel of choice for customers who *prefer* buying by phone and Web.

Some companies have products and accounts that can be sold exclusively through telesales and web channels; sometimes the economics of a business require a phone and web-based sales approach. Sales 2.0 companies with multiple sales channels leverage their sales resources and use telesales to engage their customers that like to self-educate through online resources, then want immediate access to a knowledgeable sales professional, and don't require on-site attention in order to buy. These companies encourage teamwork and collaboration but also clearly identify the roles and responsibilities of each sales organization. Sales 2.0 process and technology make this kind of coordinated approach to customers possible. Without Sales 2.0 strategy and supporting compensation, salespeople fight for the same customers, creating channel conflict.

Table 10.1 is a summary of the sweet spots for telesales and field selling opportunities for different types of customers.

TABLE 10.1   Sweet Spots for Telesales and Field Sales

	Telesales	Field Sales
Customer preferences or requirements	Real-time information Phone and online interaction and exploring on the Web Product information or trials online Relatively simple, straightforward buying process	On-site attention before purchasing Buying process has greater complexity with multiple decision makers
New business accounts	Small and medium-size businesses (SMB) Manage smaller opportunities within large companies Partner with field salespeople to close big opportunities at large companies	Larger companies or opportunities
Existing customer accounts	Renewals Upgrades and add-ons Maintenance and service sales	Customers requiring face-to-face visits whose recurring revenue justifies on-site attention

CAN YOUR PRODUCTS OR SERVICES BE SOLD BY WEB AND TELEPHONE?

While most companies selling complex products requiring multistep sales cycles can benefit from a sales development group, not every company can complete an entire sales cycle by teleselling every product. However, it's important not to assume that your company's products are not saleable by phone and Web just because they are complicated and sophisticated and have always been sold face-to-face.

Anneke can vividly recall the 1985 launch meeting for the telesales department at Oracle, now known as OracleDirect. She presented her plan to senior sales management and key field sales reps, including

Tom Siebel, who later founded Siebel Systems (now part of Oracle). Tom was one of the biggest critics. "Are you crazy?" he decried. "You'll never be able to sell Oracle by phone. Our customers will not buy complex software without a meeting." But when Siebel saw the results six months later, proving that customers would indeed make purchase decisions on the phone, he became an instant convert—and later even became one of the vice presidents to run the OracleDirect business unit himself. Sometimes the harshest critics of telesales become the most avid supporters when they see proof of how effective it is.

Implementing telesales is a very effective way to transition from Sales 1.0 to Sales 2.0. But here are some things to consider when determining whether your company can be successful with telesales:

☐   *Is your target audience comfortable buying over the phone or online?* In the technology industry, most techies are not only comfortable with an online and phone sales relationship, they often prefer it. This preference for phone and web interaction is becoming increasingly common across industries and job functions, as technologies such as e-mail, the Internet, web collaboration and conferencing, and social networking applications have been accepted by the general public. However, you must determine whether your own customers are comfortable using such methods when purchasing your product or service, in order to determine the potential success of telesales in your company. You have to sell in the way that your customer wants to buy. If you're unsure, run a pilot program.

☐   *Are you in an accepted market category?* It is not impossible to sell your product through telesales if it is the first of its kind. However, if your prospects know what you mean when you describe your product—even better, if they've used something like it and are familiar with how it works—then you can close a deal more easily without a face-to-face meeting.

☐   *Can your prospect experience the product easily?* Many customers want to try before they buy, particularly when buying by phone or Web. If your company has a liberal return policy or trial program, you can send out a product for testing and evaluation by customers. It is commonplace for software companies to allow customers to download trial software from the Internet. Today's web conferencing, product engagement, and online demo tools are so powerful that prospects can often get a good sense of your product even without a trial.

☐ *Is the entry price point of your product $50,000 or under for new customers?* There are no hard-and-fast rules, but conservatively speaking, orders under $50,000 can usually be sold by phone and web-based selling. In general, this number increases when doing business with existing customers. Some companies report that customers with whom they have trusted relationships will make purchases of any size—even millions of dollars—by phone or Web. For some large opportunities—and despite the Sales 2.0 technologies that enable remote interaction—some executives on the buying end of a large transaction still want to see a salesperson or an executive from the vendor's company in person before making a major financial commitment.

☐ *Does the decision maker for your product have the buying authority at your price point?* Lengthy approval processes can get in the way of effective telesales. It is best when your main contacts have signing authority and budget for your product or service at their level. However, there are now Sales 2.0 technologies that accelerate the sales cycle by facilitating online access to decision makers. Read about how WebEx uses its Sales 2.0 process and technology for this purpose in Part 3 of this book.

   To shorten the sales cycle, take the budget-level approval of your buyer into consideration and have telesales sell what the buyer is able to buy easily (without artificially decreasing the size of the order). A common approach is to sell entry products or services just below the typical signing authority of a single potential buyer and then sell additional products or services at a later time.

☐ *Is there an individual decision maker or a small decision-making team?* Getting one or two people to make a decision about your product can be challenging enough. It can be even more difficult—although not impossible—to sell to a large team or committee by phone and Web. But if you can get them all on the same web meeting, sales portal, or phone call, you can potentially get around this problem.

☐ *Is your product or service easily delivered, installed, and implemented?* If what you are selling is fairly simple or self-explanatory, then it is more conducive to a telesales process. However, if your customer needs complicated instructions and hands-on training to get started, an onsite visit is more likely to be a requirement.

☐   *Do you have alignment between your sales and marketing teams, and a large enough marketing budget to support a transactional sales model?* Lead generation and customer follow-up marketing programs fuel telesales. Many companies severely underestimate and underbudget for the volume of qualified leads needed to achieve telesales objectives. Your sales process conversion rates will determine how many total prospects you will need in order to generate the number of qualified leads required for achieving the telesales quota. Alignment and ongoing communication between telesales and marketing will improve the telesales team's ability to position the products, address questions and objections, and ultimately close more business.

☐   *Is your target market sufficiently large?* If you are selling to a very limited number of customers, a telesales approach may not be ideal. Telesales teams—especially those assigned to generating new business—need a large volume of targets in order to be most productive. They can make up to 100 phone calls and e-mails each day, depending on the complexity of product they sell and their ability to connect with live prospects.

In summary, Table 10.2 is a checklist to help you determine if you can be successful with telesales. If you can answer yes to most of the questions, your product is likely telesales-ready. As with any new Sales 2.0 program, run a pilot program to ensure your customers will accept a new way of buying, and you can make money with phone and web-based selling.

ASSIGNING TELESALES QUOTAS

Territory assignments, quotas, and compensation plans drive sales reps' behavior, so Sales 2.0 companies carefully design commission plans that support the company's strategic initiatives as well as what is right for their customers. This may include establishing market share with a new product launch, increasing sales into new markets or customer types, or collaborating with other sales team members to close sales in key accounts. CSO Insights' data show that companies that consistently

TABLE 10.2 Is Your Product Telesales Ready?

Questions to Ask Yourself	Answer
1. Is your target audience comfortable buying over the phone or online?	Yes
2. Can the prospect experience the product easily without a visit (e.g., with online demos or trials)?	Yes
3. Is your new business price point typically $50,000 or under?	Yes
4. Does the decision maker have the buying authority at that price point?	Yes
5. Is there an individual decision maker or a small decision making team?	Yes
6. Is your product/service easily delivered, installed, and implemented?	Yes
7. Do you have a large enough marketing budget to support a transactional sales model?	Yes
8. Is your target market sufficiently large?	Yes

drive desired sales behaviors with their sales compensation plans report significantly better results.

Deciding how telesales and other sales channels divide their responsibilities is an important, strategic decision. In order to increase customer satisfaction and sales effectiveness, Sales 2.0 includes focusing all sales organizations on customer opportunities they are best equipped to close. In companies with both field and telesales, there are three main ways to assign territory and quota: individual quota, team quota, or individual plus team quota. Regardless of option, the goal of a Sales 2.0 company is to ensure that customers of all types have proper coverage and to align sales resources with the company's goals, strategy, and culture. The result is maximizing profitability for both you and your customers.

At Blue Pumpkin Software, the cultural preference was for sales teamwork over individual accountability. Therefore, the company had a telesales model that included a shared quota with field salespeople. After an acquisition, the executives at the new company favored individual accountability, and the sales model was quickly modified so each member of the telesales team had a distinct, measurable quota and a clear responsibility for specific opportunities that were valued at less than $50,000. In addition, telesales carried an overlay quota based on opportunities worth more than $50,000 where the field salespeople would be engaged. There is no single right answer when it comes to telesales quota assignments. Rather, each one has pros and cons that need to be considered along with the company's goals and culture as well as customer preferences for buying.

Here are some examples of the different ways you can structure and motivate telesales:

- ☐ *Individual quota.* In this model, the telesales team produces revenue that is measured separately from the sales produced by the field sales organization. Their opportunities are forecasted incrementally from the field's as the telesales team takes responsibility for selling opportunity types that are different from those pursued by the field. For example, even if they are a team supporting the same customers, telesales may manage opportunities up to $50,000, and the field salespeople may be chartered to focus on opportunities above $50,000 for the same accounts. This is often referred to as a transaction bar, above which the field sells the opportunity and below which, telesales sells it.

    In a variation of the individual quota model, some telesales reps may manage all opportunities for a set of accounts that do not require or justify the assignment of a field salesperson. This is most common with small and medium-size (SMB) accounts and with customers that gravitate to information on web sites and telephone relationships with sales reps.

- ☐ *Team quota.* Telesales shares a quota with the field salespeople in their territory, and while they may close sales, the telesalespeople in this model typically do not forecast their own opportunities. A common use of this model occurs with companies that sell big-ticket items with a relatively small number of transactions. The field salespeople benefit by having an inside counterpart, but there may not be separate sales opportunities that the telesales reps can manage on their own. This model produces the greatest collaboration, and the telesales rep provides more immediate access for customers and improves the productivity of the field salesperson, though the telesales rep does not have an individually measurable responsibility for closing business.

- ☐ *Individual plus team quota.* This hybrid model gives telesales reps an incremental quota as well as a shared "overlay" team quota with one or more field salespeople. An example of this model is when a telesales rep has an individual quota based on transactions up to a certain size, or based on specific products, in addition to the opportunity and responsibility to work with field salespeople on larger opportunities. Although it creates two buckets or quotas that the telesales team needs to manage, this model provides the benefits of individual accountability, greater market coverage, and teamwork with the field on the most strategic accounts and their related opportunities while minimizing channel conflict.

Some sales organizations develop combinations or variations of these telesales models to align with their customers, products, market penetration level, and company culture. Table 10.3 is a summary matrix covering the three major telesales models and the pros and cons of each.

STRENGTHENING CUSTOMER RELATIONSHIPS WITH TELESALES

In Part 1, we emphasized that companies which follow sales process to form the most authentic, long-term customer relationships realize superior sales performance. By creating a telesales team dedicated to customers, you can develop high levels of trust with customers through regular contact and achieve benefits in terms of increased loyalty and revenue, larger order sizes, positive references, and referrals.

Customers who have experience with your company and products have different needs from those who are buying for the first time. Salespeople who are good at helping customers make an initial purchase decision may not excel at extending opportunities within an existing customer account. It also costs significantly more to recruit a new customer than to keep an existing one, and even a small improvement in customer retention can have a huge impact on profitability. For these reasons, many Sales 2.0 companies structure their sales organization with separate groups selling to existing customers and new business accounts. The new business team will typically transition their relationships to the sales team covering existing customers 3, 6, or 12 months after their first order.

Selling to existing customers is often called "farming" while selling new business is often called "hunting." At Verint Systems, where the

TABLE 10.3 Pros and Cons of Telesales Quota Assignment Types (or Models)

Model	Key Benefits	Key Issues
Individual quota	Telesales takes accountability for high volume of smaller transactions that can be sold via phone and web site Aligns field salespeople with largest opportunities Customer receives two sales resources, including one on the inside that is generally more accessible Greater market coverage and revenue	Possible manipulation of opportunities around the transaction bar that may separate telesales from field account assignment Potential field versus telesales competition for opportunities or accounts
Team quota	Minimal field versus telesales channel conflict Most collaborative approach to the customer Customer receives additional sales resource who is very accessible No need to set a transaction bar	Large quotas Telesales reps have less control over sales results compared to other models Harder to measure accountability Telesales may be used more administratively
Individual plus team quota (Telesales reps share a total or partial quota with the field and carry an individual quota)	Reduced channel conflict Compromise between individual accountability and total teamwork Customer still receives additional sales resource who is very accessible	Two quotas per telesales rep More complicated to administer Potential field versus telesales competition to double forecast some opportunities near transaction bar

typical customer has only purchased some of the company's full suite of products, the telesales team is both hunting by selling different products to the customer base or to their other divisions (which can feel more like hunting than farming since new relationships have to be formed), in addition to farming for upgrades to products the customer already has. This team works closely with existing customers to learn about their ongoing business plans and introduce new products and services that address their needs. Verint also has a field sales team focused on generating new business and closing business with large customers and prospects. By structuring the sales organization this way, the company ensures the appropriate Sales 2.0 focus on developing relationships and selling to new and existing accounts, both of which are critical to sustain business results.

Many companies depend on selling to existing customers for their growth and long-term success because of their large market share penetration, or because they sell subscription-based products or services. When a company earns more annual revenue and profit from existing customers than new customers, the development of a dedicated sales team for customers is imperative. Implementing a telesales team dedicated to customers can increase sales while enhancing customer service and coverage to protect the base against competition by preserving strong relationships and increasing trust.

OUTSOURCING INSIDE SALES

"I can't make my revenue quota unless you give me more leads!" It's a common complaint in many companies, and marketing and sales executives often respond to the salesforce's frustration by investigating outsourced solutions for Inside Sales, usually sales development. Many companies are drawn to outsourcing because they believe it costs less and is faster than building a dedicated team in-house. While companies initially save money by forgoing investments in infrastructure and staffing, the ongoing cost paid to an outsourcing vendor must be weighed relative to the results generated by the project. The key question to pose when evaluating an outsourcing decision is, "What is the ROI?" It may be more costly and take longer to hire your own people and invest in facilities and systems, but if you end up with better qualified opportunities and more sales, the investments are likely worth the time and expense.

Cost is one important consideration, but there are other reasons to consider building an internal Inside Sales program. As we've pointed out, Inside Sales provides a strategic entry into Sales 2.0 practices. The process, metrics, and levels of customer engagement possible with an Inside Sales team provide you with strong customer loyalty, critical business intelligence, and an unfair competitive advantage. Also, many field sales managers hiring new reps look to promote successful inside salespeople as their best source of experienced candidates. Do you really want to outsource such a valuable organization to an outside company?

Still, there may be some situations—for example, when piloting Inside Sales or launching programs requiring flexibility in staffing—when outsourcing can be a good solution. Keep in mind, though, that the outsourcers that invest the most in their people, process, and technology—and therefore are likely to produce the best results—are probably not the cheapest. Outsourced teleservices should not be considered a commodity.

There are also outsourcers that offer their services on a pay-for-performance basis. This pricing model sounds foolproof on the surface, but these companies do not improve salesforce productivity or effectiveness unless they deliver *qualified* leads and appointments that can be converted into revenue. Measure the results that they get paid for—typically leads or appointments—and their outcomes through the sales process steps the same way you would evaluate an internal sales development group's performance and ROI. Otherwise, you may be *decreasing* sales results by filling the pipeline with unqualified opportunities that waste the sales reps' time.

ACTEVA: EXPERIMENTING WITH OUTSOURCING AND OFFSHORING

Acteva, a leading provider of online event registration and related payment solutions, closes 99 percent of its sales without ever meeting a client face-to-face. The company even has customer opportunities worth $1 million-plus that generally buy via phone and web-based selling. From small Tupperware parties to entertainment events to major corporate conferences with thousands of people, the Acteva registration service gives customers the convenience of online event registration, ticketing, and payment handling right from their web sites.

Benjamin Nachbaur, VP Sales for North America, compares his Sales 2.0 approach to cooking. "To find the magic recipe for your sales model, you have to test and experiment." Several of his tests involved outsourcing various parts of his sales team, including sales development. The value proposition offered by the outsourcer was enticing. Benjamin recalls, "The vendor said they could scale up a team of 10 reps within a week to help us ramp up for a specific marketing promotion, and then scale back down to just one or two reps until another push was needed. That level of flexibility would have been impossible with an in-house team." However, that flexibility benefit was offset by some challenges associated with having sales development reps that were not Acteva employees. Benjamin says, "The two toughest challenges with outsourcing were transferring knowledge and ensuring we had people with the best selling skills. I've found that in-house teams are better and faster at sharing ideas and best practices. And when I hire reps myself, I have greater control over who will be interacting with our customers."

Acteva's next experiment was creating a telesales team outside the United States, in another country in North America. Benjamin hired a team of three reps in Canada who were focused on mid-market accounts, and their cost of labor was about 20 percent less than in the United States. Although that Canadian sales team performed well, it required a local manager, which quickly cut into the labor cost savings of the sales reps themselves. Benjamin believes that remote teams need a highly qualified local manager to be most effective, and generally a remote team would need at least four salespeople for the cost savings to outweigh the cost of the additional manager.

Another one of Acteva's pilot programs involved finding sales resources overseas. Frequently when people think of staffing solutions in India, they think of outsourcing. But having an internal operation in another country, or offshoring, can be a more effective option. Acteva's sales development team for general business sales is based in India, but it is made up of dedicated Acteva employees. They perform public web searches to identify sales leads, and they do not interact with customers directly. Acteva can staff four sales development reps in India for the cost of one sales development rep in the United States.

Acteva's general business sales team is another internal telesales group based in India, which consists of quota-carrying reps who sell directly to small and mid-market customers. Benjamin is happy with their performance. He says, "They do a great job. Their close rate is a little lower than what I could achieve with a team here in California, but their lower cost of sale and ability to handle a great number of opportunities outweighs the small difference we see in close rates." Since establishing the team in 2004, the revenue has grown 300 percent in three years. Also, through efficiency training and program support, Benjamin has been able to reduce the size of the team by 50 percent, while still maintaining the same exponential growth rate in annual revenue. Benjamin maintains Acteva's telesales and sales development teams that cover his largest customers under his direct supervision in San Francisco. With these major accounts, the higher cost of sale is justified by the higher close rate for new sales and renewal opportunities.

11
THE BENEFITS OF INSIDE SALES

A successful transition from Sales 1.0 to Sales 2.0 can start with building new or optimizing existing Inside Sales teams. Whether your company is an established business or a start-up, with or without a field sales organization, you can likely benefit from the Sales 2.0 practices that are part of the culture of the best-performing telesales and sales development groups. Let's consider each of these benefits in more detail:

1. *High volume:* Reach more prospects; increase and maximize revenue.
2. *High velocity:* Accelerate the sales cycle.
3. *High value:* Increase sales at lower cost by aligning resources with opportunity types and activities.
4. *Predictability:* Establish a predictable, measurable, repeatable, scalable business.
5. *Stronger customer relationships:* Communicate and engage more easily by phone and Web.
6. *Sustainability:* Reduce travel and carbon footprint.

High Volume: Increase and Maximize Revenue

Sales development reps often handle 50 to 100-plus lead generation and qualification calls and e-mails per day. Traditional salespeople generally make a small fraction of that many calls in a week, and when focusing on this type of activity, these field salespeople would be spending less time managing forecasted opportunities and closing sales. The value of the sales development team comes from engaging with prospects early in the sales cycle, identifying which prospects are most likely to buy, and increasing sales closed by quota-carrying salespeople who now have more time to do what they do best: the later sales process steps that lead to closing business.

Similarly, a team of quota-carrying telesales professionals can close substantial amounts of revenue by efficiently selling large numbers of smaller deals. Many sales organizations are giving their telesales teams more responsibility for closing business with their small to medium-size business (SMB) accounts, so that they can reduce costs while increasing the focus and volume of sales to this market segment. Field salespeople cannot physically address the numbers of accounts classified as SMB, and even if they tried, they couldn't do it cost-effectively, as the deal sizes in SMB tend to be smaller than those in larger companies. Many Sales 2.0 companies are also using telesales teams to sell smaller transactions in their large accounts, often partnering these telesales individuals with a field salesperson. They are also assigning dedicated telesales teams to stay close to customers and sell them additional products and services, as needs arise. All of these practices keep the field salespeople focused on the largest opportunities that require and cost-justify face-to-face meetings.

High Velocity: Accelerate the Sales Cycle

Sales development and telesales both accelerate your rate of new sales. A sales development team can identify and qualify more new opportunities than the field salespeople might otherwise find on their own—and they can do so in less time because that is their focus; they are compensated on developing qualified opportunities. Improving the front end of your sales process shortens the overall sales cycle and keeps your quota-carrying salespeople focused on the later, more complex stages of the sales process.

Sales development and telesales teams partnered with field sales-people can increase the responsiveness to your customer or prospect as they work together. A team is more accessible than the field salespeople alone, and Inside Sales groups are available by phone and Web while field reps travel. Although it takes some coordination, the inside and field salespeople can provide better service to the customer and move through sales cycle stages faster as a team. As we discuss in Part 4, technology can play a critical role in enabling this collaborative approach to customer relationship management.

High Value: Increase Sales at Lower Cost by Aligning Resources with Opportunity Types and Activities

Optimizing the use of Inside Sales decreases the overall cost of sales in two primary ways. First, it improves the productivity of the field sales team, leading to more closed sales in less time, which reduces the average cost of sale.

Second, since the average Inside Sales professional earns 40 to 70 percent of their field counterparts and since they perform their work without transportation, entertainment, or remote office expenses, they provide a lower cost of sale for the opportunity types they manage. You can track current Inside Sales compensation trends online at *www.sales20book.com/resources.*

Predictability: Establish a Predictable, Measurable, Repeatable, Scalable Business

Your Inside Sales organization has a positive impact on the predictability of your revenue. Because Inside Sales is a volume business, it is essential to follow Sales 2.0 practices to establish consistent sales cycle steps and track and measure them regularly. Over time, the consistent, measurable sales process that an Inside Sales team uses results in better forecasting accuracy, not only of the orders that they close but also of the disposition of leads at any stage of the sales process. This system also gives management better transparency on what is happening within the sales forecast. Because sales development is often the first point of contact for marketing-generated leads or lists, this group captures key data on the relative value of marketing expenditures. Armed with business intelligence and metrics, management can predict how scaling up the inside team will affect contacts and results in terms of conversions to sales, assuming consistent quality of performance. Speaking of performance, sales process metrics reveal the differences between outstanding sales achievers and low-performers and give managers the visibility to identify and share best practices as well as ramp up new sales reps more quickly.

In addition, a telesales team can significantly supplement your largest customer opportunities with volumes of smaller sales, and keep the field salespeople focused on the big deals. This reduces the risk of missing the company's quarterly number if one large deal is lost. By offloading many of the small to medium-sized opportunities to telesales as well as pipeline development and early sales cycle steps to sales development reps, the Inside Sales organization increases the volume and predictability of the field sales team while making its own revenue and pipeline contributions. Companies with a greater percentage of field-managed opportunities typically have fewer transactions and the widest range of quarterly results.

Stronger Customer Relationships: Communicate and Engage More Easily by Phone and Web

In addition to the benefits that Inside Sales provides to your business, sales development and telesales offer customers more choices for information gathering and purchasing. They follow the Sales 2.0 practice of anytime/anywhere engagement, supported by online resources and, in some companies, global, follow-the-sun operations. Telesales teams dedicated to customers ensure strong, ongoing relationships while generating revenue. In team selling models, telesales reps partnered with field counterparts provide better service and more attention than a field salesperson could provide alone, and the sales team can work together to come up with creative sales solutions to customer needs that may not have been considered individually. In other words, Inside Sales creates more sustainable customer relationships.

Sustainability: Reduce Travel and Carbon Footprint

While we are not looking to win the next Nobel Prize by devising a new strategy to eliminate greenhouse gases through the use of inside sales, we do promote the significant, positive environmental benefits these groups provide by reducing the carbon emissions of travel. When we consider that many onsite meetings are not truly necessary, and multiply these numbers by the size of the field sales organization and the frequency of their trips, the negative impact of travel by air or car is significant and measurable, both to financial statements and the environment. A commitment to sustainable business practices is also becoming a factor that customers consider when choosing preferred vendors. To see a full report on the environmental impact of business travel, read the "Green Guide to Your Office," written by the Climate Group and sponsored by *WebEx*, available at *www.webex.co.uk/fileadmin/GLOBAL_PDF/WebEx_Green_Guide.pdf*.

SUMMARY

Inside Sales groups are tailor-made for the strategy and practices of Sales 2.0. The benefits are proven: sales development and telesales are relatively cost-effective, leverage other higher-cost channels, and are technology-enabled, process-driven, and dependent on building rapport with customers in innovative ways. Part 3 examines how four leading companies have recognized the strategic importance of Inside Sales and how a commitment to engaging with customers, developing leads, and selling by phone and Web is a pathway to becoming a Sales 2.0 company. Part 4 explores some ideas on how you can get started with Inside Sales and other Sales 2.0 programs.

PART 3

Profiles of Four Sales 2.0 Leaders

SALES 2.0 IN PRACTICE

The world's largest enterprise software company, the global leader in on-demand applications for collaborative business on the Web, a technology start-up that developed a revolutionary approach to one-to-one marketing, and an innovative leader in the medical device field—these are only a few of the companies that illustrate Sales 2.0 principles in everyday practice.

Oracle Corporation, now a multibillion-dollar enterprise, made a bold transition from a traditional enterprise-only selling strategy when it incorporated Sales 2.0 practices over twenty years ago. This move earned the company a universally recognized reputation as a sales and marketing giant. In spite of its size, Oracle continues to exemplify the kind of sales innovation typically associated with a much smaller company.

WebEx Communications, acquired by Cisco in 2007, catapulted to global leadership in its field through unparalleled ongoing marketing programs and a cutting-edge Sales 2.0 selling team that showcases its on-demand products.

Genius.com, a young, venture-funded start-up, accomplishes more with its small sales team than many companies double or triple its size, by following process-driven sales management and empowering sales reps with enabling technology.

Syneron produces next-generation medical devices. Its visionary CEO recognized that by investing in a reengineered sales strategy, he would gain a major competitive advantage in his relatively traditional industry.

Read their stories, and be inspired.

ORACLE®

genius.com

Syneron

12

ORACLE CORPORATION: THE ORIGINAL SALES 2.0 COMPANY

ORACLE

O racle, the world's largest enterprise software company, has always been a sales and marketing leader. In the 1980s, Oracle stunned the investment community with year-over-year double-digit revenue growth, due to its aggressive sales organization and recognized product excellence. I once asked CEO Larry Ellison, "What is the urgency? Why do we have to kill ourselves for unprecedented growth?" Larry explained, "It's a matter of survival. The window is now, or we'll be gone in ten years." True to Larry's words, Oracle turned out to be the leader among enterprise software competitors, many of which no longer exist. Oracle, one might argue, was the original Sales 2.0 company. It innovated the notion of integrating a multichannel sales strategy, sales productivity, processes, and technology with best-in-class people to overperform in a competitive, growing market.

Since its inception, Oracle has been known for hiring risk-taking visionaries. The company's sales leaders are not only excellent performers, but they are also smart, creative, strategic thinkers who are always looking to improve productivity and results. As a result, the company built a sales organization that embodied Sales 2.0 principles early on—during an era before the Internet, let alone Web 2.0 technologies. From the outset, the company shifted from a traditional, direct field-sales-only approach to include indirect and other distribution channels, as product, market, and customer buying changes made it unprofitable to sell the same old way.

THE BIRTH OF SALES 2.0 PRACTICES

One of the initial drivers of change was Oracle's release of its first product for small computers (PCs) in 1985. Before then, Oracle was known for its relational database technology for minicomputers such as Digital Equipment Corporation's PDP-11 and VAX models. The average selling price (ASP) for the Oracle product designed for a minicomputer was $48,000. For a PC, the Oracle product's ASP was $1,000. To make the cost of sales acceptable—and to implement a new go-to-market strategy to quickly address the new high-volume market—the company needed a different sales strategy and infrastructure. Priced at $1,000, the lower-margin PC Oracle sale didn't warrant the field sales organization's time and cost. Besides, field sales was given incentives to handle the big opportunities, not small deals.

At the same time as the PC product release, Larry Ellison ventured into what turned out to be another winning sales and marketing strategy: demand generation marketing. With the help of advertising wizard Rick Bennett, the first campaign was launched. The objective was to invest in marketing programs that would produce consistent volumes of inbound leads for the salesforce by using a combination of direct-response advertising and direct mail. Rick's edgy style was a good fit for Larry's brazen nature. His web site introduction claims, "I create predatory ads that put you on the map . . . and permanently disable your competition." The campaign was aimed at the market leader, Ashton-Tate, and it depicted an F-15 Eagle fighter shooting down the enemy German World War II–era biplane. The call to action was to phone Oracle on the 800-number hotline to learn more about the product on the PC. This is what the ad looked like (Figure 12.1).

Figure 12.1   Oracle's First Advertisement

Courtesy of Rick Bennett (*www.rickbennett.com*).

The ad was clearly effective in engaging customers, and the response it evoked was overwhelming. It generated an immediate onslaught of incoming telephone inquiries. Despite the obvious excitement that ensued from such a strong response, Oracle realized immediately that something had to be done about organizing and setting priorities for all these sales leads.

Soon after the advertisement ran, Oracle introduced a third business-changing milestone. The company changed its product packaging and pricing strategy and unbundled—or separated—its various product offerings in order to provide more flexibility to customers, rather than forcing them to license the Oracle database along with the entire toolkit of available Oracle products. This new strategy addressed the needs of the market and lowered the price of entry for customers, while simultaneously providing new and ongoing revenue opportunities for Oracle in its customer base.

During this time, I was in charge of designing a new sales organization for Oracle to address the recently available market of opportunities that were created by these business-changing initiatives. We needed to find ways to speak to three separate groups: the volumes of new buyers for the lower-end products, the existing customer accounts (installed base) who might need upgrades or additional products after their initial order, and inbound telephone callers who were responding with interest to our new marketing campaigns. We would communicate with these new buyers via the only cost-effective medium available at that time: the telephone. Thus, in 1985, OracleDirect—then named Corporate Sales—was launched.

THE FOUNDING OF ORACLEDIRECT

OracleDirect—which is now considered the Ivy League of Inside Sales—was originally conceived as a sales support function for the field sales reps. Shortly after OracleDirect launched, though, it became apparent to us that customers were willing to make purchase decisions without face-to-face sales calls. Because of this development, I recommended structuring the group to include sales reps who performed two distinct functions: telesales (to close sales) and sales development (to educate, qualify, and nurture opportunities before turning them over to a salesperson). Quota-carrying salespeople have different strengths and skills from lead generation specialists, and our consistent inbound call volume justified separating the functions.

With the strategy, organizational structure, and infrastructure plans in place, many at Oracle began to realize that OracleDirect could be perceived as a threat to the all-powerful Oracle field sales organization. So with Oracle's senior sales management's support, I rolled out a small pilot telesales program. In order to gain quick adoption, the beta test region was chosen carefully based on its proximity to headquarters, and the openness and acceptance level of the field sales reps in the local region. Field sales organizations are often intimidated by a telesales program. A discord can cause poor communication and account coordination, and a general lack of cooperation.

Sales revenue and profitability increased more substantially for the region that supported the pilot. Based on these results—which were presented at the company's quarterly sales meeting—the entire Oracle field sales organization subsequently requested a rollout for each region. The pilot program became a standard process for regional (and later, global) implementation at Oracle and has become a best-practices methodology in Sales 2.0 companies.

With the whole field sales organization on board, telesales reps were organized by the same territories that existed in the field—including Major Accounts, Federal, and Resellers. OracleDirect was centralized in one office at the company's headquarters in the San Francisco Bay Area, and it became the fastest-growing organization in the company in its first year. It contributed $6 million in incremental revenue at the highest profit margin of any sales group within Oracle. Equally important was the fact that OracleDirect affected the sales productivity for the entire salesforce by offloading the smaller business prospects and deals from field sales and delivering the high-priority, qualified leads needed to double the revenue number attained in the previous year.

By the third year, the group was contributing almost $15 million in annual revenue, with consistent monthly sales. In fact, we never missed our numbers. Craig Conway (former CEO of PeopleSoft, acquired by Oracle), who at that time oversaw my group in addition to strategic partner sales groups, used to say that the telesales group was a money machine. He'd say, "I look at their quarterly quota and know I can take the money to the bank, unlike my other sales groups where making quotas is dependent on closing one or two big deals." The individual reps' quotas were around $1 million per year, selling a high volume of orders of $50,000 and under on a single purchase order. This included new business sales, as well as sales to the Oracle customer base.

Unlike the telesales group, sales development was not organized by territory and did not carry a revenue quota. These reps had qualified lead quotas instead. They responded to and tracked the direct-response marketing and advertising programs that generated large volumes of inbound calls. Sales 2.0 metrics and processes were born in this organization, which Oracle's database system strongly supported. The group used Oracle's in-house technology to maintain a disciplined sales process to gather and enter customer data—which resulted in automated lead ranking and electronic distribution to the appropriate field or telesales rep. In addition, literature fulfillment—all of which was done by U.S. mail at that time—became automated, as did the reports requested by marketing to measure ROI on demand generation marketing programs.

SALES AND MARKETING ALIGNMENT AND COLLABORATION

The alignment and integration of marketing and sales at Oracle was always a critical success factor of the new sales model and Sales 2.0 principles, which allowed us to measure and compare the ROI of different campaigns. Marketing and sales managers and employees alike had incentive bonus programs, which offered strong financial rewards for meeting measurable quarterly goals. Since marketing employees were evaluated on how effective their programs were in generating qualified opportunities, they worked as partners with OracleDirect to carefully track the sources of the incoming leads and assign to each one a ranking of A, B, C, or D. The product groups—which were compensated on sales of their products—were motivated to conduct product training to ensure that the sales presentations were accurate and appropriate in exploring and meeting customer needs. The integration and cooperation of marketing and sales, supported by performance goals and compensation, are critical components of a Sales 2.0 company.

Senior-level leadership is also critical when shifting to a Sales 2.0 culture. Oracle's chief executive, Larry Ellison, acknowledges the importance of interdepartmental cooperation. Claims Ellison, "Functional directors—aka department managers—do a good job of optimizing business processes inside their own functional areas: marketing, sales, service, manufacturing, accounting, HR, and the rest. Functional directors have no authority to optimize processes between and across functional areas. That's why things break down between marketing and sales. . . . Only the CEO is responsible for the business as a whole. If the CEO doesn't connect the dots, the company will never operate efficiently" (Matthew Symonds, *Softwar*, New York: Simon & Schuster, 2003).

RECRUITING AND TRAINING A SALES 2.0 ORGANIZATION

In 1985, the challenge that I faced was to hire a sales group that was consistent with the company culture that Larry Ellison had created. Mike Humphries, an early sales executive at Oracle, remembers that when he wanted to hire an assistant who was an experienced secretary, Larry told him not to. "It's easier to teach a smart person to type than to teach a good typist how to be smart," Larry said. I followed this advice in hiring entry-level sales professionals. I couldn't attract seasoned sales veterans like those we had in the field, as they wouldn't have glamorous field sales jobs with lavish expense accounts; they would work at their desks and be on the phone all day. The word "telemarketing" was terribly stigmatized, and in 1985—unlike today—Inside Sales was not an almost universally accepted sales channel for technology products. So I had to get creative in recruiting the best and the brightest to my new sales department.

This challenge did not deter our chief sales officer at the time, Mike Seashols. Mike went out to lunch one day at TGI Friday's, came back to the office, and said, "Anneke, I have the perfect candidate for your first telesales rep." "Great, Mike! Who is it?" I said enthusiastically, thinking he would recommend an experienced sales professional he used to manage at his former company, IBM. (Mike has such amazing sales skills that he could even make an entry-level telesales job sound appealing to such a person.) Mike told me, "It's the waitress who just served me lunch. She's perfect."

Now, Mike taught me almost everything I know about selling, and I have great respect for him and his keen ability to recognize talent.

But a TGI Friday's waitress? Give me a break! I humored Mike, though, followed up on the interview—and discovered he was right. This waitress—Stacey—was a bright, fun, personable UC Berkeley English major who had been working in a restaurant while looking for her ideal postcollege job. As usual, Mike sensed correctly that Stacey was someone who would excel in the Oracle sales environment. She became the top-performing salesperson as the group grew.

The formula for success was hiring smart, ambitious, but inexperienced sales staff, who were motivated to learn new things and who were unwilling to fail. This was one of the keys to Larry's staffing strategy of "intellectual egalitarianism"—attracting talented employees to all levels of the company and promoting successful overachievers rapidly. He'd say, "Because of our growth, the administrative assistant or entry-level employee you hire today will be managing a department in six months." And that was true—as evidenced by my own experience. In 1980, I started at Oracle as the company's twelfth employee; and as a Stanford grad, I left my ego at the door. In my first job, my primary responsibility was answering the phone. I was an administrative assistant to multiple people, and I learned a little about accounting, sales, and software development. And true to Larry's word, I was promoted within months.

Sally Duby, now my right-hand woman in her role as President and COO of Phone Works, remembers her own similar situation: "Before joining Oracle, I was a senior sales executive selling computers and computer peripherals, but Anneke hired me to start in an entry-level job as a telesales rep, so I could learn the software industry. I was fortunate to have several opportunities for promotion during my OracleDirect tenure. First, I was regional telesales manager for the East, and then I headed up the sales development group. I really benefited from Oracle's policy of promoting from within."

In 1985, people in Silicon Valley were hearing good things about the opportunities in the burgeoning software industry—and Oracle in particular. The Silicon Valley buzz worked to my advantage in our recruitment strategy. College graduates dreamed of joining Oracle, and our telesales group was a popular choice for nontechnical candidates. The hiring environment then was very different from today's. There were few, if any, experienced telesales reps available to hire—especially with any complex software industry experience. We didn't have a training program in place until years later, so the first people hired into OracleDirect had to be bright and self-motivated enough to learn not only the product but also how to engage and sell to Oracle's customers in creative new ways. A leveraged compensation plan consisting of 50 percent guaranteed or base salary and 50 percent commission at quota helped motivate high achievers, who could earn even more by reaching "stretch goals" above their quotas.

What were the best sources for this type of raw talent? Due to our location in the San Francisco Bay Area, we sought graduates from Stanford and Cal (UC Berkeley), resulting in a profile that was a perfect fit. As the years progressed and Oracle became better known, we attracted sales candidates with rich sales training experience from the likes of Xerox and IBM. My first manager in sales, Craig Conway was originally skeptical about hiring English, history, and philosophy majors instead of business graduates, but he soon learned that the best, most open-minded Inside Sales performers were often liberal arts majors.

Oracle's sales training is now something of legend. As formal programs were launched, OracleDirect reps learned side-by-side with the field, where sales and technical training was being implemented. This strengthened both their knowledge and their relationships. A full-time training staff—which collaborated with field sales and product management subject-matter experts—was later added to the inside group. This training staff was and is a critical investment in delivering and reinforcing product, sales, and process skills training.

In today's Sales 2.0 world, a rich and growing community of qualified and experienced telesales reps in many industries has received training at previous companies. At the speed of today's business, it would be risky and costly to depend on an entirely new team of inexperienced reps. However, implementing a hybrid team of junior and experienced talent often proves to be cost-effective and successful, especially given young people's affinity for online communications.

INTEGRATING TECHNOLOGY, AUTOMATING PROCESSES

Thanks to Oracle's strength as a leading provider of business software, OracleDirect was a technology-enabled business from the start. In 1988, the original in-house Oracle sales application no longer suited our needs. I recruited one of the company's talented, up-and-coming technologists from our consulting division to create a more robust implementation of

Oracle for our internal use. Kevin Kraemer joined OracleDirect to build OASIS (Oracle Automated Sales Information System), which is now recognized as the precursor to the Siebel CRM System. OracleDirect also adopted electronic mail early on, and used it internally to distribute qualified leads and reports to the field salesforce. Even in the late 1980s—a relatively rudimentary period of sales-specific technology—Oracle was out ahead of the pack, using the strength of its products and an orientation to automation to transform itself into an early Sales 2.0 business. Today, the next-generation tools of the twenty-first century have further strengthened the Sales 2.0 principles within the company and improved both efficiency and collaboration.

Perhaps more importantly, the process-oriented engineering approach to sales, the separation of sales steps and assignment of different sales stages to people with varied jobs and skill sets, the recognition that different kinds of buyers require different selling and interaction methods, the use of marketing to drive a consistent volume of leads into the sales pipeline, and the consideration of using the lowest-cost sales resource while maintaining high-quality customer engagement are quintessentially Sales 2.0. These qualities have been embedded in Oracle Sales since the 1980s. As Larry Ellison says, "I believe that every process within an organization—marketing, sales, service, everything—should be carefully engineered. This can be done only if a company implements systems that automate and monitor its business processes. I'm still an engineer at heart, but now I apply engineering discipline to our entire business, not just product development" (Symonds, *Softwar*).

ORACLEDIRECT AND SALES 2.0 TODAY

Observing OracleDirect today is akin to watching one's once-precocious child enter adulthood as a wise and seasoned veteran. Rudy Corsi, Senior Vice President of OracleDirect and Operations, tells me, "If OracleDirect were an independent enterprise software company, it would rank as one of the largest and fastest-growing software companies in the world." Now 1,600 employees strong, the renowned Inside Sales operation is slated to generate over $750 million per year in revenue, while also qualifying leads, moving them through the sales cycle, and contributing to total company sales that are ultimately forecasted and closed by the field and other sales channels.

Though we believed in the 1980s that we were selling a complex set of technical products, we had a pretty simple product catalog compared to Oracle today. Essentially, we sold Oracle database technology, some development tools, and consulting and support renewal services. Nowadays, Oracle has acquired dozens of companies and sells thousands of products to thousands of different types of customers. And managing this myriad of sales and buying processes is immensely complicated.

SALES ORGANIZATIONAL STRUCTURE MAPPED TO BUYERS

With the explosion of product offerings, the company's sales resources—both inside and in the field—are organized by product category. The company has followed Sales 2.0 practices to address the differences in buyer types and sales processes for Oracle's business applications products—those that support operations such as sales, finance, human resources and manufacturing—versus Oracle's technology products. In North America, in addition to having separate sales divisions for each product category, there are also divisions for different sizes of companies. The NASA (North American Strategic Accounts) group covers top-tiered accounts; the Mid-market group covers accounts under $500 million; and the Commercial group handles companies in between the two. To cover different time zones in North America, the OracleDirect organization has expanded to include several hubs outside of headquarters, including Boston, Toronto, and Sandy, UT, near Salt Lake City. Additionally, the San Jose and Minneapolis offices are centers of sales expertise for specific products, having been added with recent company acquisitions, including Siebel, PeopleSoft, and Hyperion. This approach to organizational structure, customized to the needs of customers, according to product, customer size, customer type, and location, is today's Sales 2.0 industry standard.

TEAM SELLING REDUCES CHANNEL CONFLICT

Since my era, there has been a dramatic shift in the division between what the telesales and field groups sell. Telesales' revenue restriction of

$50,000 is long gone; today, OracleDirect reps and field reps share a territory and determine together—on a deal-by-deal basis—who will manage each opportunity. An OracleDirect rep could sell a $500,000 deal if it can be closed by phone and Web. On the other hand, if customers won't place a $40,000 order without a field visit—and if they are valuable enough clients to warrant a face-to-face call—the field rep manages the deal. OracleDirect reps' quotas vary, depending on the products they sell, but in general, they carry $1.5 million annual quotas or more. The field rep partners' quotas include their own revenue target as well as the corresponding OracleDirect rep's quota. Both OracleDirect and the field get paid for everything that closes within their shared territory, but they are each awarded a higher commission rate on deals that they close themselves.

Oracle's collaborative team selling, Sales 2.0 technology–enabled approach really works for them, their market, the products they sell, and their customers in today's technology world. The field sales organization's culture has shifted from one of channel competition with OracleDirect to one of respect and cooperation in building customer relationships. After over 20 years of coexisting with a telephone and web sales organization, Oracle field sales has grown to embrace and promote the competitive differentiation of OracleDirect, the company's Sales 2.0 showcase.

Distinct roles, responsibilities, and territories, however, are more important when introducing a new Inside Sales channel, unless your sales culture is unusually open-minded and your field reps have had positive experiences with inside groups. Oracle in the 1980s was not so evolved. In the first year of my OracleDirect management tenure—after we rolled the program out to all U.S. territories—some field sales reps complained about telesales calling into their accounts, despite the fact that during the launch phase, we paid the field the same commission rate, regardless of who closed the deal. This circumstance highlights issues beyond financial remuneration, such as account control, that have to be addressed when launching a new Inside Sales program. The early program allowed the field to have holdouts—accounts that were deemed strategic and needed management by field resources. An example was a *Fortune* 500 account that was evaluating Oracle technology for a company-wide implementation, but was testing the first system on a PC. Although the initial deal size was small, the field wanted to manage the account because of its very large potential beyond the first order. Some field reps took advantage of this loophole, though. There were some accounts that were reserved as strategic even without obvious follow-on business opportunity. I spent a lot of time negotiating with my counterparts in the field, especially Gary Ketelsen and Danny Turano, VPs of the Western and Eastern regions, respectively. "Danny," I'd say, "you can't tell me that this $15,000 deal is strategic! That's a telesales customer!" Known for his great sense of humor as well as his talent in deal making, Danny used to tell me, "Of course it's strategic! It's strategic to my field rep's commission check!" And therein lay the problem. If field reps needed just one small deal to hit their next accelerator and earn a higher commission rate, they'd argue to slip a small deal into their forecast, even when it was better for the customer and Oracle for the deal to be managed by phone.

There were even times when a telesales rep and a field rep would compete for the same customer. Deals right around the $50,000 mark had the potential to become smaller or larger, depending on the manipulative tactics of the Oracle sales rep—and regardless of the customer's best interest. As we uncovered situations like this, it became clear which reps were cooperating with the intent of the program and which reps were bending the rules for their own selfish benefit. The smartest, most successful field reps figured out right away that they could make the most money and attract the best customers by focusing on the biggest deals, and allowing telesales to make money for them in the background by closing the small and midsize accounts or smaller orders in the bigger accounts. In a way, the introduction of the telesales channel was the fastest way to leverage the high-performance field sales reps while weeding out the weakest ones, who tended to cling to every sales opportunity—even the smallest ones that could easily be managed more cost-effectively.

Every program has its glitches at the start; fortunately, most Oracle telesales/field teams currently operate in a mutually beneficial partnership that best serves the customer. If a customer opportunity that a telesales rep uncovers grows and requires field management, the field partner is more than likely to replace it with a deal he or she has been managing to keep the telesales rep's forecast whole. Even so, some opportunities still evoke competition and require management intervention—typically in territories where the relationship between the field and telesales rep is weak—but today's channel conflict isn't enough of an issue to warrant placing arbitrary limitations such as deal size on telesales and field reps. Instead, Sales 2.0 managers focus on relationship building and collaboration with company peers as well as customers. As I was staffing the original telesales organization, I attempted to ward off the field/telesales conflict problem, which typically stemmed from lack of trust, by inviting field reps and managers to interview the telesales reps joining their regions. Once the field feels that they have a say and have bought in to someone sharing their customers, fewer issues with channel conflict occur.

Still, integrating field and telesales channels requires thought and analysis, and Sales 2.0 companies with multiple channels of distribution like Oracle fine-tune the program every year. In the 1980s, we analyzed our business and customers every quarter and tracked and measured the company's deal flow, volume, average sales price, and profitability at different price points annually, which helped us define what telesales should sell from year to year.

THE INTERNET CHANGES COMMUNICATIONS

Technology breakthroughs that buyers adopt change businesses. Sandy Bruce was managing the OracleDirect organization in the mid- to late 1990s when the Internet became an integral part of communications in the business world. She implemented a new group, Internet Response, to address the growing number of buyers that wanted to interact with Oracle not by telephone but over the Web. The majority of Oracle's customers were technology-savvy, and their preferences were changing quickly to take advantage of the new medium. Being a Sales 2.0 organization, OracleDirect evolved its telephone-centric model to include the Internet. With the help of her technical team, Sandy also took the next step in using technology to enable the sales process. She discovered that there was a small company called WebEx that had a remarkable product, which allowed sales reps to share information visually on a computer screen with prospects during a telephone call. Oracle was a beta customer for WebEx, which was a start-up at the time.

"The product opened up all kinds of new opportunities for us, both in OracleDirect and the field," Sandy says. "Anything that you would show a customer in person—such as a slide show or product demo—you could now show on a computer screen." She recalled a turning point when she convinced the field of the power of this new medium and recounted the following incident: "We offered a webinar for CIOs (chief information officers), a sought-after audience for many of Oracle's technology products that has become very hard to reach. Jeff Henley, then Oracle's CFO, was the keynote speaker, and he gave the presentation right at his desk. No one had to travel to attend. We ended up attracting several hundred highly qualified buyers with that event. And as they entered the session, we could see who was in attendance," Sandy reports.

Sandy also emphasizes the importance of systems, tracking, and measurement: "I had a dedicated data center in my group because of the importance of the reporting and tracking systems. We needed to stay on top of daily activity metrics, because without understanding the trends, we couldn't make our quota. Telesales is a very consistent business. We sold products every day, every week, every month, and if some key metric was off, like qualified lead volume or a conversion rate from one sales-cycle step to another, I needed to know about it. It's not like the field, where I came from, where you could swoop in with one large deal at the end of the quarter and make your number."

ORACLE PRODUCES SALES 2.0 LEADERS AND ENTREPRENEURS

There is a long list of very talented individuals who came through OracleDirect and made major contributions to its evolution over the years—some of whom are very well known in Silicon Valley. One of these people is Marc Benioff, whom I hired right out of college. He started his career at Oracle in the telesales organization before being promoted within the company, and eventually leaving to become Founder and CEO of salesforce.com. Tom Siebel, Founder and former CEO of Siebel Systems (acquired by Oracle), also managed the group for several years after starting at Oracle in the Chicago field sales office and then running strategic sales efforts for Oracle. Hilarie Koplow-McAdams, now Executive Vice President of Global Corporate Sales at salesforce.com, made major strategic contributions during her management tenure in a period of rapid expansion and new business initiatives.

Like me, Hilarie started at Oracle on the "ground floor." What has struck me as I've interviewed the current management of OracleDirect is how similar the Oracle employee profile is to when I was at the company from 1980 to 1990 as well as how many of the division's stars have been promoted from entry-level positions.

Erica Ruliffson is a perfect example of this consistency. Currently Group Vice President of Oracle's CRM OnDemand Sales, Erica started as a telesales rep in OracleDirect in 1995. Though the group now almost exclusively hires reps with several years of sales experience, they made an exception with Erica. A Spanish and Latin American studies major at Dartmouth College, Erica says, "I felt a little funny about taking an entry-level sales position and wearing a headset when all my Ivy League friends were joining glamorous-sounding investment firms." Thirteen years and several senior management positions later, her career has taken off—and she has no regrets. She appreciates the extensive learning involved with coming to Oracle without industry background through the training she received, which she instantly put to use on the phone with over fifty customers per day. She believes this experience was a perfect foundation for her career, and provided her with a solid understanding of the heart of Oracle's business from the frontlines.

ORACLEDIRECT INDIA STRATEGY

Before leaving OracleDirect for the CRM OnDemand Sales group, Erica was part of the management team that implemented OracleDirect's India strategy. In 1987, at the height of the India outsourcing craze in the high technology industry, Oracle's Chairman and then-CFO Jeff Henley asked the OracleDirect management team what its India strategy was. It was a question that he was asking many groups within Oracle, given the potential for cost-savings benefits. The team proposed that the OracleDirect India operation be an in-house group of newly hired Oracle employees rather than an outsourced team to handle back-office, behind-the-scenes sales support. At launch, the OracleDirect management team's charter was to recruit 16 sales consultants who would design proof of concept custom demos for qualified prospects that could be delivered by a North American OracleDirect rep over the Internet.

Additionally, Erica experimented with adding an outbound sales prospecting function in India. She needed to test whether the North

America market would have any issues accepting sales calls from contacts in India. Due to the presence of other technology companies in Bangalore—including IBM and SAP—the city has become a hub of deep technical expertise. The sales development reps—called business development consultants (BDCs) at Oracle—who work out of that office are highly competent technical people, with special expertise in middleware and SOA (service-oriented architecture). Oracle's technology customers' major requirement for engagement is technical competence, so technical buyers have no problem conversing with the Indian BDCs. Oracle considers this group to be a great fit for the database and technical products portion of the business. The BDC group's charter is to make targeted follow-up calls to lists, including those contacted through customized e-mail marketing campaigns and prospects who have downloaded information or products from *www.oracle.com*. At 500 strong—a number that includes 100 sales consultants—the OracleDirect India operation is today a major Sales 2.0 organization selling to small Oracle accounts by telephone and Web.

BRINGING SALES 2.0 PRACTICES TO ORACLE APPLICATIONS CUSTOMERS

Selling Oracle applications—the complex software packages that automate business functions like manufacturing, finance, human resources, and sales—is another story, though. Erica found that the OracleDirect India organization's deep technical strengths didn't work especially well when engaging prospective customers for Oracle's applications products, who tend to be businesspeople rather than technical experts. In addition, she learned that cultural differences could be more of an impediment for these business prospects than they had been for technical prospects that OracleDirect India reps contacted. Therefore, the majority of those interested in Oracle applications are contacted by a BDC organization in one of three North American cities—Toronto, Minneapolis, or Sandy, Utah—which are OracleDirect's hubs of applications expertise—while technology buyers are called by BDC reps in Bangalore.

Lane Monson, Group Vice President of OracleDirect applications, runs the sales development and telesales operations for the enterprise resource planning (ERP), customer relationship management (CRM), and other Oracle applications sales. Lane is another entrepreneurial sales manager, who came to Oracle in 1998 after 10 years in IBM field sales and sales management. His initial role at Oracle was selling and then acting as a product specialist for CRM applications in the field sales organization. But he was recruited into OracleDirect by Hilarie Koplow-McAdams to help determine how, and *if*, the inside group could sell Oracle applications.

During the late 1980s and early 1990s, I had fairly low expectations for Oracle sales managers—who had only field sales experience—to be able to perform a management job in Inside Sales. The skills required to manage an inside operation—with its technology-friendly orientation, high volume of sales calls, and focus on metrics and processes—were often very different from those of the average Oracle field sales manager. But as Sales 2.0 practices are taking hold across sales cultures, field sales organizations in every industry are integrating technology to engage with customers and are adhering to processes to reduce cost and increase efficiency. Furthermore, in a company like Oracle where there is a 20-year history of the field and OracleDirect partnering to communicate with customers, forward-thinking sales managers like Lane have embraced OracleDirect's Sales 2.0 practices as a critical piece of the company's sales culture.

Lane had something unique to offer OracleDirect, which was an organization with very little experience with applications sales. In the past, there was a preconceived notion within Oracle that it was impossible to sell applications without a face-to-face visit. In fact, Jeff Walker—who started the applications business at Oracle during my tenure—told me flatly that his products could not be sold by phone. But Lane had an advantage. He was a trusted member of the field sales community with a history of success selling applications, chartered to experiment with what was possible by phone and Internet. Lane credits field sales senior vice presidents John Boucher, Matt Mills, and Mark Johnson, and their field sales teams with embracing and acting as champions for the integrated model of selling Oracle applications.

Lane tells me, "The first thing we had to do was look at the metrics and the sales process that were proven for the technology side of the business, and figure out what if any of that infrastructure could be applied, adapted, or changed to create an applications sales business within OracleDirect." The technology sales reps sell database and tools software to technical buyers, while applications sales reps sell primarily to business buyers looking to make their departments more effective and efficient. Lane found that it was indeed difficult to sell an initial order for applications products without visiting a customer; only about 15 percent of their sales are new license sales. But by building a skilled inside salesforce with experience selling application software, Lane designed a very effective business strategy based on creating long-term relationships with Oracle applications customers after their initial purchase. His Sales 2.0 account management team follows up with key customer contacts via a defined process using phone and e-mail to discuss the customer's business changes and requirements. In discovering a buyer's company has expanded or developed new business needs, they sell additional user licenses, upgrades, new product modules, and new subscriptions. The account management model is used effectively to remain engaged with customers and sell them additional products and services of any price. This brings increased sales productivity and reduced field sales costs, as field reps close new business deals faster knowing that OracleDirect continues to uncover additional opportunities.

OracleDirect applications reps do a small amount of travel—typically two to three trips per year—to see their customers and meet with their field rep counterparts. Because there is a career path from OracleDirect to the field, this creates an opportunity for the telesales reps to enhance their skills and learn from their field partners. In this way, the Inside Sales team keeps relationships with customers and field reps strong by supplementing their primarily telephone and web-based communication with occasional face-to-face visits.

Adherence to sales process and methodology are fundamental Sales 2.0 best practices in Lane's sales organization. OracleDirect's sales steps are an adaptation of those created for the field by InfoMentis, Inc., a sales methodology company. WINNING Inc. and Corporate Visions, Inc. are also key sales training partners of OracleDirect. Best practices are tracked and measured religiously and shared throughout the organization. Lane can link his team's success to the following core competencies: continuous improvement, hiring of top talent, superior installed base selling, and understanding Oracle's internal business processes. The key metrics tracked—in addition to license revenue—include ranking of reps, number of transactions, average transaction size, number of customer interactions, number of opportunities uncovered, and dollars of pipeline created. Speaking of metrics—in six years, Lane has grown the OracleDirect applications business from a staff of 32, mostly filling orders from the field, to 230 people generating revenues of $250 million. In addition, Lane's applications BDC team generates qualified leads for the field that will result in over $150 million in incremental revenue.

SALES 2.0 OUTSIDE OF THE UNITED STATES

The successful Sales 2.0 practices exemplified by Oracle are not just an American phenomenon. The OracleDirect model has been replicated successfully all over the world. Before taking a senior management role with OracleDirect in North America, Erica Ruliffson pursued an opportunity of her dreams: to work abroad. Given Erica's Spanish-speaking skills, she sought out and attained a position at Oracle in Argentina, working with Sebastian Gunningham, then the managing director. Sebastian had been considering starting a telesales group to complement the field salesforce, and had been looking for someone with experience. After several interviews via videoconference, Erica was hired. Soon after, her new manager was promoted to run all of Oracle's Latin American business.

Oracle's implementation of an international business strategy early in its history was another key to its success. Larry Ellison hired John Luongo (who later became CEO of the Vantive Corporation) in the 1980s to head up Oracle's international business division—a move toward global thinking that was pioneering in the 1980s. By the end of the decade, over half of Oracle's worldwide revenues came from non-U.S.-based customers, served by nearly ninety subsidiaries and distributorships. In its first three years, OracleDirect was so successful and instrumental in Oracle's rapid growth that the group caught John's attention, as well as that of the executives running Oracle's subsidiaries outside the United States. John, like many Sales 2.0 leaders, wanted to introduce innovative sales programs that had proven successful in the United States into the international business model in the spirit of sharing best business practices internally. He recruited me to work with him on that initiative and focus first on telesales and sales development efforts.

Oracle's international management was much decentralized in those days. John's approach was to hire the best entrepreneurial leaders possible and give them ultimate decision-making control regarding how to best manage their organizations for timely and effective results. He did very little in the way of corporate mandating, as long as the managing directors delivered their numbers. Participation in the new sales programs was strictly voluntary, even though we knew from our experience in the United States that the revenue and profit implications of Inside Sales were substantial.

Oracle U.K., the Netherlands, Australia, and Canada signed up right away. I became an internal consultant to help them implement pilots and roll out programs customized to their local markets that were based on the American OracleDirect model. Oracle Hong Kong, Mexico, and several European subsidiaries saw these first-year results and followed suit the following year—adding tens of millions of incremental dollars in high-profit revenue.

Erica's international experience came at a different time in the company's evolution, since by 1998 the tide had swung toward globalization and centralization. Once the regional pilots were proven in Latin America, Sebastian decided that it was more cost-effective to have one organization serving all subsidiaries in the region than to duplicate infrastructure and staffing in multiple countries. Oracle Europe's management had already made this decision and established headquarters for OracleDirect Europe, in addition to other functional groups, in Dublin, Ireland.

The hub chosen for Latin America was Miami, and Erica was asked to start up the new group. Because accents and business knowledge are specific to each region, Spanish and Portuguese speakers hired in Miami could not call into every country credibly, which would cause the program effectiveness to suffer. So Erica needed to recruit native sales teams and relocate them to Florida. Within a year, she had found and outfitted new facilities, recruited 30 people from countries all across the Latin American continent, and put all the resources in place to launch Ligna Directa, the OracleDirect of Latin America.

During its first year, Ligna Directa was universally well received by the field sales offices. There were only a few telesales reps for each country, so quotas were not increased and the field reps were paid on telesales deals. The marketing managers appreciated having a sales development organization that was well trained in consistently track-ing the results of their demand generation activities. Erica's background in the OracleDirect process meant that everything was measured. For years prior, the field sales organization had struggled to capture simple metrics such as lead volume and conversion of leads to sales. Dur-ing Erica's management, Oracle's CRM product—newly acquired from Siebel—was implemented in Miami to support her group's activities. It was one of the product's first implementations in the company; before any customer or Oracle field office installation.

Sebastian (who has since become a senior executive at Amazon.com) was impressed with these first-year results, and directed Erica to scale the group from 30 to 100. This kind of growth brought the assignment of a more substantial quota. In an effort to motivate the field to sell larger deals, customers licensing products $50,000 and under were assigned to telesales in the larger regions. In smaller countries, telesales sold deals $25,000 and under. In time, as telesales proved that they could meet customers' needs and sell more business by phone and Web, that bar was raised to $150,000. With this increase in responsibility came the first signs of tension from the field.

Over the initial two years, the managing directors and their teams were asked to make some major transformations. Previously, every coun-try had its own data center, support, and marketing organizations—even their own web sites. The last sacrosanct function that the country man-agers owned was sales, and now even that was being seized by "a bunch of kids" in Miami who were calling into their accounts and carrying 30 percent of their quota. Even double compensation doesn't make up for this perceived loss of control and pride of ownership in forecasting business. Erica spent a lot of time during the ramp-up phase of the pro-gram on the phone and traveling to each office to address issues and concerns. Her language and relationship-building skills were imperative in preventing mutiny in the field.

And, despite the protests, the new model made a lot of sense for Oracle and its customers. Telesales was the perfect channel for Latin America's SMB market, which is characterized as high-volume, low-order-size. It also worked well with the Oracle customer base—mostly oil companies and banks that had no compunction placing $100,000 technology product orders through the phone and web channel. With these two market opportunities covered by their telesales partners, the savvy field reps got comfortable with the ample additional opportunities elsewhere in their territories.

After some initial consternation over the new sales development function interfering with their accounts, even the veteran country managers who had initially met the process with some resistance came to appreciate the new sources of qualified and prioritized sales opportunities that came from Oracle's now-centralized demand generation marketing programs and professional lead qualification group—especially after Erica published some early success stories. What was initially perceived as a threat was eventually recognized as a valuable resource.

Centralization also worked beautifully for another key part of the Oracle sales process: sales consulting. This group of technical experts supports the sales function by answering customers' technical questions, designing custom demos, and responding to requests for proposals (RFPs). With the organization established in Miami, sales consulting resources could now be shared across the region. Taking the sales consultants out of the field and putting them in the Miami hub made them much more efficient. No longer were they on the road constantly, being monopolized by a handful of field reps. Instead, they were accessible through a hotline and supported by technology, and they started turning around deliverables for customers of the field and Ligna Directa alike. The sales consultants were organized by product expertise—such as database technology or middleware—and were therefore able to serve many more Oracle customers much faster. In a traditional field office model, you lose that kind of economy of scale. This hub of experts is a Sales 2.0 model that OracleDirect has duplicated successfully around the globe.

Erica's success in bringing these Sales 2.0 principles to Oracle Latin America in the late 1990s show that innovative sales practices *do* work outside of Silicon Valley. In perhaps one of the least likely cultures on the planet—one where personal relationships rule—there was a natural and good fit for Inside Sales processes. The perception that Latin American business leaders uniformly want to sit across the desk from an Oracle sales rep just wasn't true. Just as in the United States, these executives appreciated the choice they had to engage with Oracle in another way—one that was more respectful of their time than the traditional manner of doing business. Erica had heard laments about it being impossible to sell the complexity of Oracle's product set when she first introduced the program to the Latin American field team; one managing director wanted to set the revenue bar at a very restrictive $7,000. But having support from Sebastian—the region's most senior executive—made all the difference. He made sure the managing directors cooperated. Erica reports that in her day, about 40 percent of the region's revenue came from the telesales channel with an ASP of about $15,000.

In order to stay competitive, Sales 2.0 businesses have to keep evolving with market changes, and international business has the added complexity of foreign currency, exchange rates, and language considerations. In the late 1990s, the value of the dollar was so high that it became too expensive to continue operating a centralized group from the United States; the subsidiaries simply couldn't afford the charge-backs. So the model was fine-tuned to adapt to changing economic conditions. There are now four separate hubs in the largest Latin American subsidiaries: Brazil, Argentina, Mexico, and Colombia.

Oracle Europe went through a similar transformation. As in Miami-based Ligna Directa, OracleDirect Europe, headquartered in Dublin, included a multilingual staff from every country on the continent. Country-specific toll-free numbers were featured in local marketing campaigns and routed to the sales team speaking the appropriate language, so that customers believed they were calling in-country. As Dublin became a popular headquarters choice with many companies—due to the advantageous tax benefits offered by the Irish government in exchange for establishing a local presence—competition for employees increased, and costs rose. Inside Sales reps felt limited in their career path opportunities as well, since promotions to the field required relocation. For these reasons, OracleDirect Europe was decentralized into about five language hubs in the early 2000s.

GLOBAL COLLABORATION AND BEST-PRACTICES SHARING

Collaboration and sharing of best practices are characteristics of Sales 2.0 organizations, and Oracle displayed these traits early in its history. As Oracle rolled out successful new sales initiatives outside the United States in the late 1980s, I organized regular meetings of sales managers worldwide to share experiences and results—and discuss what worked and what didn't—in an effort to compile best sales practices for the company. The first of these meetings were for inside and field sales managers in the first countries to adopt the new sales model. While Erica was still an Inside Sales manager in Latin America, she continued this practice by creating a global steering committee for leaders of all Inside Sales operations worldwide. These biannual meetings included representatives from Europe, Middle East, and Africa (EMEA), the Asia-Pacific region, and India. One of the observations Erica made was that while the model was fairly consistent, the needs and interests of sales managers with new programs differed a lot from those with more established groups. For the first year or two, for example, the managers' issues were basic and included compensation strategies, sales process, fundamental technology implementation, and organizational structure. Concerns with advanced metrics management and the deployment of more sophisticated technologies came later, after a sales team had tested and fine-tuned basic processes. This parallels what happens in any organization adopting new Sales 2.0 programs such as Inside Sales, whether it is an established company implementing a new initiative or a new company launching its initial sales strategy. This is why it's important to start with defining and understanding the basics first: sales strategy; hiring, training, and compensation programs; metrics, processes, and systems. Once an organization is more mature and these fundamentals are established and tested, advanced Sales 2.0 technologies are more easily integrated and are more likely to improve sales productivity and effectiveness.

TECHNOLOGY INNOVATIONS ENHANCE THE SALES PROCESS

Vice President of Sales Consulting Norm Gennaro, who joined OracleDirect in 1996, remembers how technology enhanced the way the group sold. "At first, we were simply having a phone conversation while showing a PowerPoint presentation over the Web. The idea was to give customers something to look at while we were talking to them, just to help with their comprehension of the technology." Given the fact that Oracle is full of talented and creative technical people like Norm, the technology rapidly reached another level. Norm was encouraged by his manager, Hilarie Koplow-McAdams, to develop in-house Oracle products to help reps increase sales productivity and effectiveness.

Guided Selling was one of the first technologies that Norm's team created. Built as a web site inside Oracle, it provided a platform that assisted reps in explaining products visually to customers while they were on the phone together. At the same time, it served as a basis for product training, reinforced consistent messaging for each product, and was instrumental in OracleDirect's expansion and sales growth, by providing sales tools such as recorded webinars (online seminars), scripted presentations, embedded demos, guides with key phrases to use to describe products, and customers' Frequently Asked Questions (FAQs).

Guided Selling provided these benefits without the constant involvement of a sales consultant to help explain a product's technical capabilities. It was a tremendous way to leverage the knowledge of the relatively small number of sales consultants available to support the salesforce and its prospective customers. While the ratios between sales reps and sales consultants change regularly, and are different in every Oracle sales division, there are approximately ten sales reps to every sales consultant in OracleDirect. Therefore, Norm had to find a clever way to stretch his group resource. Technology, in the form of Guided Selling, was his answer.

Guided Selling was so important for customer engagement that OracleDirect management tracked its usage and related metrics closely in its initial years to help understand the sales cycle and the steps that buyers were taking before making a purchase decision. Specific sales metrics could be tracked, such as the percentage of times reps sell products in addition to the Oracle database. Today, Norm explained, there is less need for Guided Selling in OracleDirect in North America, as the group has evolved and largely moved upstream in terms of the complexity of their sales. OracleDirect has adopted an enterprise selling strategy that is more closely aligned with the field's method, rather than volume selling one or two point products to single, mid-level decision makers. However, Guided Selling may well be an important technology for OracleDirect India, as the group moves from being strictly a sales support group to a selling organization.

Another key technology that Norm's team developed—and that the OracleDirect sales consulting teams regularly use—is a web-based demonstration server called Solutions Factory. It's described to customers as "see your business in our software," and it allowed Oracle Sales to make a Sales 2.0 move from a position of pitching products to stepping into the customers' shoes. Norm tells me, "We didn't want to just demo our products, and we wanted to hear what our prospect's business was all about. So using our resources, our business intelligence and portal software, and our servers, we'd deliver a custom system prototype using Oracle web collaboration software. The prospect didn't have to do anything—no software installation, no downloading, nothing—except explain their problem or need and supply their data. It was a fast, scalable way to showcase what we could do for customers. It was especially effective for the mid market because larger companies usually have the resources and expertise to build these prototypes themselves."

Solutions Factory is still used today in OracleDirect, but it has morphed over the years into a sales information portal and communications hub for customers. Norm explains that the sales reps give users a URL (web site address) and a personal ID number (PIN) to access the site and communicate with their sales rep. They can look at a variety of tools and documents like RFPs, self-running demos, screen shots, industry articles, or details on support contracts. Through a whiteboarding application, they can share information on the fly, and the visual component helps reps to see exactly what the customer needs, which is key to forming the basis of a trusted relationship. The login information provides Oracle with tracking information about usage, which helps determine the specific interests and level of engagement of the buyers.

All of this tracking information, the lifeblood of OracleDirect, along with the base Oracle CRM system, is summarized in a sales portal—and gives OracleDirect's sales operations group the metrics or key performance indicators (KPIs) that drive the group's productivity management. KPIs include activity and conversion metrics for each rep, such as call and qualified lead volume, custom demos, and marketing and web conference activities. The tracking of these leading indicator activities and how they affect the sales cycle is fundamental to Sales 2.0. As metrics management becomes more and more sophisticated, advanced technology becomes more of a requirement.

In OracleDirect, customer engagement and collaboration with other members of the sales team are enhanced through extensive use of Instant Messenger (IM) in the sales process. When companies like AOL and Yahoo! made chat functionality universally popular and useable outside the company firewall, sales reps gravitated toward IM communications in conjunction with their other tools, especially to strategize with sales consultants or subject-matter experts during a selling situation. Norm says, "IM is a huge part of our lives today, and I can't imagine a sales call without it."

Lane Monson contends that even Oracle's advanced internal use of its own CRM product falls into the category of Sales 2.0—given the company's ability to execute customized marketing programs that match prospects' interests. Because of Oracle's standardization on one centralized system, departments including marketing, sales, support, and contracts all have a coordinated view of the customer or prospect—including their installed products and how they are using them as well as the interaction history between multiple contacts within Oracle and its customers. With this extensive account knowledge, OracleDirect's BDC reps can continually build on relationships, add to the profiles while prospecting, create customized lists, and perform highly specialized outreach campaigns to discover new opportunities. Marketing's efforts are coordinated with the OracleDirect and field sales organizations as well; before implementing demand generation campaigns, the groups collaborate to determine priorities and suggested targets.

Web Diagrammer is another popular internal sales tool, used to create pictures of a customer's IT environment, including applications installed, facilities in which they are located, and the divisions the products support. This information has proven invaluable to customers and Oracle sales reps alike, who work together to keep the data current. The records are integrated into Oracle's internal CRM system and used as a road map to track installation information and discuss ongoing additional opportunities with customers.

TECHNOLOGY IMPLEMENTATION AND ACCEPTANCE: TAKE AN INCREMENTAL APPROACH

Considering the complexity of Oracle's sales-enablement technologies, one imagines that there might be some issues with implementation and performance. But Oracle is fortunate; since the company is a major software developer, the company has access not only to world-class products but also to technical talent to support the internal systems. "The good news," says Norm, "is that Web 2.0 technology makes it so much easier than it would have been in the past. We can create a wiki or blog using all standard open source technology, putting all the pieces together in a way that makes sense for our sales reps, our customers, and our business. The technology we are using now is literally off the shelf and anyone can build what we've built."

User adoption, on the other hand, is a bit more difficult. As Norm explains, "The biggest challenge is never a technology challenge; it's getting the users to understand the value of the technology and incorporate it into their daily work." Norm believes that although OracleDirect uses Web 2.0 technologies extensively, the sales reps—the majority of whom are not technical people—don't need to know how the information on their portals is being consolidated from multiple servers using Web 2.0 technology, whether it's an RSS feed or XML. They just want technology that helps them do their jobs better, by providing easy access to the data and effective ways to communicate with customers without travel.

Sales consultants—the geeks of the sales organization—tend to gravitate more to technology for technology's sake. But they too are using Web 2.0 tools in creative and empowering ways to assist the sales cycle. Norm recounts how the group has evolved with available technology. "When I first started, we had a hotline staffed by sales consultants. When OracleDirect reps needed to get an expert on the phone, they would call the hotline number; then I would get on the call and address the customer's technical questions and issues. When the number of sales reps grew and there weren't enough sales consultants to go around for every call, the group initially found relief by staffing up the India operation. But now Oracle's product set has not only increased in volume, it has also dramatically increased in complexity. It is impossible to be a technical expert on all the products." So once again, Norm turned to Oracle's own products (Application Server and WebCenter Suite technology) for a solution, and used them to create a blog that allows sales reps to feed in their questions or issues (which mostly come in by e-mail now, instead of by phone). The blog is actively managed by a set of knowledge workers that ping sales consultants around the world—from North America, to India, to EMEA, to Asia-Pacific—when a question comes up that's related to their expertise and skills. So instead of having one person on the phone trying to answer all questions—and thereby risking possible inaccuracy and timeliness—the blog/wiki is finding the best person in the Oracle organization to address the customer questions as they arise. Norm explains that one expert's knowledge pales in comparison to the collaborative expertise of a community of experts.

In fact, *New Yorker* columnist James Surowiecki discusses the advantages of this approach in his book *Wisdom of Crowds.* Accuracy inevitably increases when a large number of people—the "crowd" or the community—are interacting with the system, adding to it, and improving it in real time. And the sales reps get their answers quickly because there is a dedicated group managing the system. Norm explains, "a good example of the wisdom-of-crowds concept is the lifeline feature on the game show *Who Wants to Be a Millionaire?* In his book, Surowiecki reveals that when contestants have the opportunity to ask for help in answering a question, they receive the best answers not from calling one smart friend or family member; but rather from asking the audience."

The only challenge that Norm initially faced with the introduction of the knowledge-sharing blog in regards to his technical staff was an employee motivation issue within his sales consulting group. "Technical people like to be recognized for their expertise and specialized knowledge, so sharing that across the worldwide organization required a different mindset. A lot of sales consultants initially felt that putting their answers up on the Web and sharing them publicly diminished their value to the organization." Management has to be ready to address change in an organization when it's not always comfortable, and must remain aware that there is a culture shift going on.

Norm adds, "Senior management has to appreciate the vision as well, and we have been very fortunate that Larry (Ellison) has always supported and celebrated all the innovation that came out of this group." To alleviate discomfort in the user community, Norm suggests taking an incremental approach to Sales 2.0 technology implementation— especially with sales reps. "Constant improvement and advancement works. You have to be somewhat subtle about the changes you make. Maybe add a few new features at a time, so not everyone notices. Then perhaps one of the top reps mentions, 'Have you seen this? It works great!' and it becomes a viral adoption, rather than Big Brother making a mandate."

WHAT'S AHEAD? ORACLE'S NEXT-GENERATION CRM PRODUCTS

As a Sales 2.0 pioneer in innovative sales practices and technology, Oracle is already delivering the next generation of products addressing sales productivity. They are focused this time on individual reps and their social relationships with customers. Anthony Lye, Senior Vice President of CRM, is raising the bar with his next set of products, which changes the paradigm for sales enablement tools. Anthony claims, "The version 1.0 CRM systems automated the old pencil and paper forms that sales reps once used to record contact and account information. These applications are great for management reporting and account tracking. But for the most part, they don't help reps sell more."

Traditional CRMs have been a critical foundation for implementing Sales 2.0; without them, sales managers couldn't track customer interactions and perform the basic measurements that allow them to understand and predict their businesses. However, Anthony's next-generation CRM tools take the next step to enhance each individual rep's productivity and ability to create relationships with customers. These applications make the user experience more intuitive by bringing to the forefront the social, partnership-style connections between sales reps and customers. The new "CRM 2.0" release includes capabilities that allow sales reps to access easily all kinds of changing information about their customers from outside sources, including news feeds and profile updates on social networking sites. It will also improve collaboration and sharing of customer information across departments.

Oracle's innovations in technology and sales practices stem from the culture of its CEO, who is always looking ahead to continually improve on the status quo. In the words of Larry Ellison, "Don't tell us how you've been running your business for the last 20 years. Instead, let's try to figure out how you want to run your business for the next 20 years." (Symonds, *Softwar*). Spoken like a true Sales 2.0 leader.

13
WEBEX COMMUNICATIONS: SOFTWARE-AS-A-SERVICE LEADER AND SALES 2.0 SHOWCASE

V ice President of Cisco WebEx Worldwide Sales and Service, David Berman, tells us that he calls one of his favorite sales presentations "Death of a Salesman." Exuding passion and enthusiasm for his job, David says, "This pitch is all about the demise of the old way of selling." The sales model he brought to the company when it was a year old is widely regarded as one the most successful and innovative in the industry. It is based on the fundamental philosophy that communicating with customers by Web and phone can be more efficient and just as effective as solely selling face-to-face.

The name WebEx is practically synonymous with collaboration, web meetings, and webinars the way Kleenex is with tissues. The company is the global leader in on-demand collaborative applications and the number-two software-as-a-service company in the world. Fitting the "network as a platform" strategic vision, WebEx was acquired by networking giant Cisco for over $3 billion in 2007, 10 years after its founding, when revenues were $380 million.

WEB-TOUCH SALES

David and his Inside Sales group—or "web-touch sales", as they call it at WebEx—had no small part in building this kind of skyrocketing value for the company. The fact that WebEx's sales are driven by hundreds of reps using Sales 2.0 technologies and methodologies should not be a surprise, given the web meeting software and on-demand collaboration tools that WebEx sells. These are some of the most universally used enabling products that make Inside Sales so effective, and make it possible to share information visually while on a phone call. They are dead simple to use: all you need to get started with the product is an Internet browser and a phone. Through online demos, presentations, and webinars using their own products, WebEx sales reps easily engage customers and give them a sense of how they could use the products in their own environments. David calls this the "online demonstration center."

While mature Sales 2.0 companies like Oracle started with a field-oriented Sales 1.0 strategy and later added the Sales 2.0 process-driven Inside Sales team, more and more software companies today—especially those with on-demand licensing models serving the SMB market—are launching with an Inside Sales–dominant, Sales 2.0 approach. WebEx is a great example of this new generation of companies. For a number of reasons, telesales is the preferred sales channel for many companies that offer their products via a subscription or on-demand basis. Vendors of on-demand products can reach a large number of prospective clients quickly without needing to go onsite to perform extensive installations and training. They can stay in touch with their user base and manage accounts without traveling. And from the customer's perspective, it is easy to try out the product without making substantial commitments in terms of employee or financial resources. Thus, the SaaS market is ripe for phone and Internet interaction.

As the size of WebEx's customers grew, the company added a field sales organization to the mix. But since WebEx's fundamental philosophy was based on Sales 2.0, it continues to be a leading innovator of sales strategy and process. However, some challenges along the way in implementing its methods have driven this world-class sales organization to continually improve productivity.

Reminiscing about his own sales career, which began at Xerox and ADP, David emphasizes that his success at the company came from a learn-as-you-go approach, especially when facing setbacks and disappointments. David admits, "We made many mistakes, and there was learning at every stage." Some early sales professionals, who had formerly been field reps, had to undergo a transformation when they joined WebEx. "They had to shift away from jumping on an airplane every time they found a qualified prospect and learn how to conduct a lot of their business by phone and the Internet." One San Francisco Bay Area–based rep, who couldn't break the habit of scheduling face-to-face meetings with his customers all over Northern California, struggled to meet quota—until he moved away from the area, stopped traveling, and began using the Web.

There was also a time when David had difficulty convincing some new sales managers, whose global accounts team sold to WebEx's top 500 customers, that even very large companies are willing and eager to communicate in nontraditional ways. When they reorganized the group using a traditional enterprise field sales–only approach, sales decreased. David retrained the global accounts reps to use the web-touch method of selling in addition to onsite visits, which led the team to meet its quota for the next six quarters in a row.

USING WEBEX TECHNOLOGY AT EVERY STAGE IN THE SALES PROCESS

At WebEx, successful sales reps and managers "eat their own dog food," according to David. By walking around the WebEx sales floor, we see that sales reps talking to prospects have the WebEx Sales Center site up and running on their screens. Many have web cams, so they can further personalize interactions and give prospects a face to the voice. Reps use WebEx at every stage of the sales cycle. Prospects who click on a link in an e-mail invitation experience WebEx presentations online when they attend a webinar. Sales reps who follow up afterward by phone can schedule a WebEx demonstration on the fly. When technical questions arise, reps are able to find a subject-matter expert anywhere in the world who is online at that moment and available to join a call. Contract review and negotiation are also done in real time using WebEx, which allows all parties to edit a document together. Between meetings, reps can use the WebEx sales portal to make files, meeting appointments, presentations, web site links, or recorded webinars available to the prospect, and then determine what has been downloaded, by whom, and at what time. It is easy to understand why customers and sales reps alike are enjoying the instant access to information and speed at which business takes place when they utilize these technologies. Figure 13.1 shows the WebEx sales portal.

In addition to increased productivity and reduced cost of travel, another important benefit is associated with using WebEx products. In an age of increased concern about global warming, customers and sales reps using WebEx can feel good about consuming far less fuel than

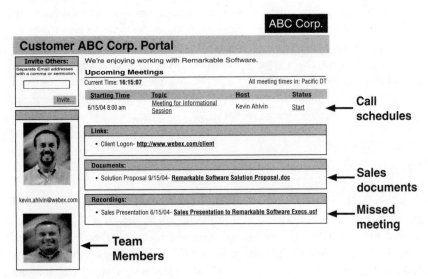

Figure 13.1   The WebEx Sales Portal

what is needed for the airplane and automobile trips associated with traditional face-to-face selling. WebEx's Work Green program promotes the reduction of CO_2 emissions by taking meetings online. Claiming, "One businessperson saves 2,690 pounds of carbon dioxide by moving a sales presentation online. One person flying from New York to London equals 2,690 pounds of carbon emissions," the WebEx web site invites prospects to use a carbon calculator to see how much damage they're doing to the environment with business travel.

SALES ORGANIZATION STRUCTURE BY FUNCTION AND CUSTOMER TYPE

Due to the massive volumes of incoming leads that WebEx's marketing group generates, David created both a nonquota-carrying lead qualification (sales development) group and the web-touch selling group, which closes sales. Leads generated through the Web are automatically scored according to a prospect's title, function, company size, and readiness to buy. Qualified prospects, or "A" leads, are routed to the appropriate web-touch sales rep while the remainder stay in sales development, giving this group the chance to further nurture and manage the leads with ongoing marketing programs.

WebEx boasts sales offices of at least thirty people all over the United States, Europe, Asia, and Australia. Its Santa Clara headquarters includes a start-up team with Spanish- and Portuguese-speaking reps covering Latin America. David is also exploring outsourcing parts of his business to India.

One of the programs that David's sales development group uses very effectively to further spark the interest of prospects is called the "Daily Demo", which WebEx created years ago, and has since been adopted by many a software company. Daily demos are offered multiple times a day and are structured to be small and interactive, so buyers can ask questions specific to their business and situation.

WebEx's sales territories are organized by customer type into four segments, based on geography and size of company: Global, National, Small and Medium-Size Businesses (SMB), and the newest, Small Office/Home Office (SoHo). The lion's share of WebEx's sales come from SMBs, which are defined as companies with 750 and fewer employees. SMB reps carry annual quotas of close to $1 million. Their average sales cycle length is "subthree weeks," and the top reps close seventy sales per quarter—or more than a deal a day.

For each geographic territory, there is two-person team consisting of new business reps ("hunters") and customer success reps ("farmers"). The customer success group begins to contact customers 90 days after they download a product to confirm their satisfaction with WebEx. While the main goal of that call is to make sure the customer is having a good experience with the WebEx product, it also provides an opportunity for the reps to build stronger relationships with their customers, get to know customers' business goals more intimately, and find additional needs within accounts that might require WebEx solutions. Customer success reps who identify new product or service opportunities pass these leads to their new business rep partners and are rewarded with a referral bonus, rather than a traditional sales commission, when deals close.

INVESTMENT IN PEOPLE

David is a big believer in developing his people and promoting from within. A natural career path exists for reps to move from sales development into an entry-level sales position on the SoHo team (which handles smaller orders), and from there to territories consisting of increasingly larger companies. Says David, "About 40 percent of my sales development reps are promoted into sales every year."

A training budget of approximately $1 million per year supports continuous learning and career development. Training at WebEx is not a one-time event. The company has a five-day orientation training for new hires in sales, but there are multiple short training sessions every week or two as well. Training is considered an ongoing process, including professional sales training, which is delivered to the WebEx salesforce by M3 Learning Corporation. WebEx emphasizes operational, day-in-the-life style training that reps can implement immediately on the phone or Web with customers. And as one would expect, much of WebEx's training is delivered online, using WebEx products.

The WebEx sales organization prizes innovation, and David looks to the people closest to the customers—his sales reps—for new ideas. "If something is working well, we transfer best practices to other members of the sales group by sharing success stories during our team meetings," he says.

MARKETING AND SALES: PART OF THE SAME PROCESS

As impressive as WebEx's sales machine is, it would not thrive without the equally top-notch marketing machine that feeds and drives it. Jeff Weinberger, WebEx's resident guru on its Sales 2.0 initiative, is also in charge of marketing for WebEx's sales solutions. Jeff spends a lot of time thinking about creative ways to engage his buyers and "start a conversation." He fills us in on how they think about marketing at WebEx: "Sales has always been about the relationship with the prospect, but there's a lot that happens before and after a lead first interacts with our sales group. In Sales 2.0, you have to manage that relationship from the very first time someone hears about you, which could be from a web site or an e-mail. There are communities of people out there that are readily accessible online that are influencing how your prospects perceive your company and your product. Our job in marketing is to understand and, if possible, influence that perception of our reputation and presence in the market.

"Another part of Sales 2.0," Jeff continues, "is knowing the customer's buying cycle. In marketing, that includes how we get customers interested enough to decide they might like to buy from us. And that also starts long before they talk to us. We're not just looking to fill the sales funnel with any old prospect names and phone numbers; we're looking to create an interest in buying and bring qualified prospects into the funnel. At WebEx, the sales and marketing processes are truly integrated and interdependent. Sales and marketing work together; we are all motivated and compensated to create customers out of potential buyers."

Given WebEx's strength in marketing—particularly to a very large market of small companies—consider what it takes to be successful in the multibillion-dollar SMB market. WebEx's investment in marketing says it all: the company spends close to $100,000 per SMB rep per year—about the same as their on-target earnings (OTE)—to generate leads for the salesforce. This makes WebEx a kind of nirvana for sales reps: they never have to cold call.

WebEx does a fair share of traditional marketing as well, such as brand advertising in magazines and events. They also do search engine marketing, but it's the online "content campaigns" (e-mails offering free, educational white papers and webinars) that create most of the demand—to the tune of hundreds of thousands of leads per quarter. "The reality is that if we offer information that's interesting and useful, people show up, and that opens up the opportunity for interesting conversations and new customers," maintains Jeff.

A great example of a content campaign is the company's webinar series. In 2007, WebEx offered one or more webinars a month just on sales effectiveness, including web-touch selling. The company runs five to ten per week on all topics. I signed up for one of the webinars and experienced firsthand how the advanced, automated, tightly managed marketing process at WebEx works. Since roughly half the people who sign up for events actually attend them, WebEx has e-mail routines to confirm registrations. This process also allows WebEx prospects to add the event to their calendars, remind them before the event, thank them afterward and give them an opportunity to engage further with the company by purchasing a product, getting a free trial, downloading a white paper, or taking another action. Various e-mails are tested and tracked to determine which ones get the best responses from different kinds of audiences.

A similar automated process is triggered when requesting a white paper. After I filled out an online screen that captured my name, e-mail address, phone number, and qualifying information (including title, company type, and company size), I immediately received this e-mail, inviting me to engage with the sales rep:

Anneke,

Thank you for your interest in WebEx. Please find the links to the white paper(s) you requested below.

Improve Your Sales Process Using Web Conferencing
www.WebEx.com/pdf/wp_sales.pdf

From my research, your company may be in a great position to leverage web collaboration solutions. I would like to understand your business objectives and determine how WebEx can help you meet them.

Can we schedule a time for a brief discussion of your business needs? Please reply with a date and time that works for you.

I look forward to hearing from you.

(Name of WebEx Rep)
Solution Specialist—WebEx Communications, Inc.
3979 Freedom Circle, Santa Clara, CA 95054
Sales_rep@WebEx.com

In addition to the campaigns planned and executed by marketing, WebEx sales reps act as territory business managers and send their own ad hoc, personalized e-mail campaigns directly to their prospects and customers. Because the sales team has the best sense of which leads are most promising, these contacts typically receive follow-up calls first.

Jeff is using his creative and experimental nature to pilot some never-been-done-before campaigns at WebEx that can only be described as Sales 2.0. They include the multimedia WebEx Sales Makeover, which he describes as the "first online Business-to-Business reality show." In conjunction with *Selling Power* magazine, he has created a white paper, videos, specialized landing zones, e-mail campaigns, print awareness, and a custom web site. In the series of webisodes—inspired by the ABC show *Extreme Makeover: Home Edition*—WebEx professionals help company CEOs improve their sales performance using WebEx products while selling.

WebEx's cross-departmental organizational structure also exemplifies the Sales 2.0 philosophy of functional alignment. Sales, marketing, customer care, and channels are all aligned by territory. There is one leader for each of the four segments: Global, National, SMB, and SoHo. "Because we're so closely aligned," says Jeff, "we really think of marketing and sales as one process at WebEx." Jeff explains how marketing and sales work together. "We have segment managers, aligned with the four sales teams, who own the marketing budget for their team. Their job is customer acquisition through marketing programs for their sales segment, such as SMB. This is similar to how it's done in companies selling consumer products." Jeff continues, "So if I want to run a program, I have to develop ideas that are tailored for each segment and convince the segment manager that it will generate good results. This keeps me accountable and focused on producing qualified leads and proving ROI for every single campaign that I create. Otherwise, I might not get the budget to run the program, and I'd miss my goals for getting my products into the marketplace."

THE IMPORTANCE OF PROCESS, TRACKING, AND MEASUREMENT

WebEx's approach leads to meticulous tracking and constant improvement in marketing programs, another marker of a Sales 2.0 business. Jeff knows, based on historical data, that if he spends a certain amount of money to run a particular kind of program, he can expect a given number of responses with a predictable cost per lead. He can also foretell almost to the penny what revenue results the company will produce based on the qualified lead volume. "It's really no different from any other investment in the company where you look at your cost of capital and compare it to the return," says Jeff. WebEx's finance group, also part of the functional alignment, is intimately involved with marketing in setting cost-per-lead targets based on the profit margins that the company needs to meet each quarter.

Rigorous adherence to tracking and measuring also exists in sales, and makes it possible for WebEx to predict quarterly results with startling accuracy. The person responsible for the groundbreaking, innovative sales process and measurement at WebEx is Vice President of Solutions Sales Stu Schmidt. Stu has spent an entire career thinking about and implementing improvements in selling. Stu joined WebEx in 2004, after over 20 years of running his own consulting company and acting as chief sales officer for multiple others. He brought an unparalleled, metrics-oriented discipline to the company's sales process. Stu says his process improvements have paid off: productivity, as measured by the average number of deals closed per rep per quarter, doubled.

How did Stu do this? First, he defined the sales process from the perspective of the *customer's buying process,* one of the fundamental philosophies of Sales 2.0. Then he used his consulting background to analyze the existing sales approach at WebEx to determine where improvements in efficiency and effectiveness could be made. While the problem for most companies is having too few leads, WebEx had the opposite challenge. The company needed a process to help them prioritize the constant stream of incoming leads that its powerful marketing engine generates, and to address them quickly.

The WebEx sales process is based on the major phases that a typical sale goes through, and consists of six key steps, culminating in a seventh step: the order. This road map to winning deals includes:

☐ The critical activities to be done at each step and who is responsible for each of them.
☐ The corresponding steps the *customer* takes in the buying process.
☐ The sales tools to be used at each step (e.g., checklists, slide decks, account, qualification, negotiating and closing plans).
☐ The verifiable outcomes, which include agreements between or actions taken by *both* the WebEx sales rep and the customer. These can only be achieved when the sales rep has clearly understood the customer's business concerns, what they are trying to achieve, and the quantifiable business value they expect.

Figure 13.2 depicts the process.

While a measurable, repeatable, scalable sales process is the holy grail in managing a sales operation, Stu laments that most sales leaders measure the wrong things. "You can't manage sales merely by measuring outputs. You need to track the typical activities in your sales process that give rise to verifiable outcomes or measurable results. Measuring numbers of calls or average length of call, for example, is not particularly helpful. Counting the number of qualified opportunities added to the pipeline, on the other hand, helps us measure progress through the sales cycle."

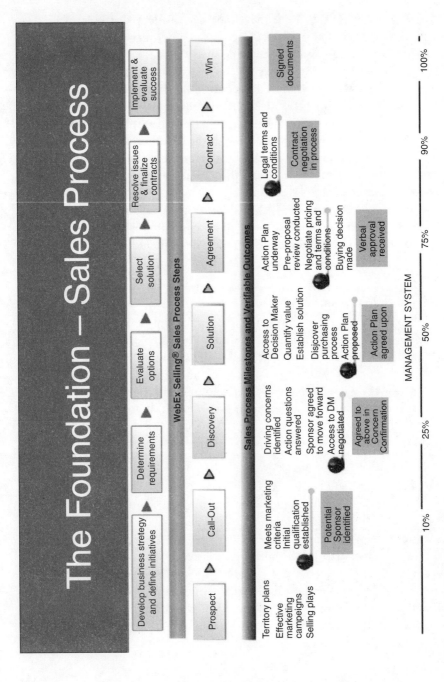

Figure 13.2 WebEx Sales Process

144

IMPROVING KEY METRICS: SALES CYCLE LENGTH AND CLOSE RATES

Stu specified goals of shortening the WebEx sales cycle and improving close rates, and then identified two key areas for improvement within the sales process: identifying the buyer type and gaining access to the decision maker. Through his "buy/sell alignment" process that he had used in his former consulting company, Market-Partners, he developed qualification questions to be used early in the sales cycle to help determine key buying styles—commodity versus value buyer, and product versus solution buyer—and how to best sell to each of them. Commodity buyers make their decisions based on things like features and functions, price, and availability, while value buyers need to understand a bigger picture of how a unique product or service will relate to their company's business objectives. You can't pitch a feature/function-oriented commodity solution effectively if the buyer has no idea what he needs. On the other hand, presenting complicated solutions and quantifying business value to a buyer who is just asking for price and availability won't work either.

"This distinction between commodity and value buyers is not new," Stu admits, "but in Sales 2.0, there are additional buyer types that have to be considered. If your customer knows how to solve his problem, he is a product buyer. If he is open to direction, he is a solution buyer. You have to sell to them differently." Stu gives us some examples. "A typical product buyer is an information technology person who needs to implement a computer network and can specify exactly how many routers, switches, firewalls, and gateways he needs. A typical solution buyer is someone investigating e-learning for the first time because his competitors are doing it, but he either doesn't know where to begin or doesn't have the time to make it happen." Moving buyers from commodity to value and from product to solution typically results in an increase in average selling price, but this is only possible by asking questions—not by pitching solutions. Stu explains, "You can determine a customer's buying style in five minutes if you know the right questions to ask. This can save you two weeks in the course of closing the deal. Understanding not only the buying process *but also* identifying the buying style is fundamental in Sales 2.0. You can't sell in a way that's different from the way the customer is buying."

To help reps gain access to the decision maker—which is a key verifiable outcome—Stu came up with seven major methods, including a WebEx buyer-specific action plan. This plan, which Stu designed to get the client working with the sales rep to make a deal happen by a target date, spells out a time line and set of actions required *by each party*—not just the sales rep—for a purchase to happen. Stu explains, "We tell our contacts that these are the actions that we need to take jointly in order to get to the outcome they're looking for. One of the required actions is having a conversation with the key business decision maker. Once the prospect agrees to this, we count that as one of the activities we track and measure."

"CUSTOMERS DON'T BUY SOLUTIONS"

Stu is famous around WebEx for making the seemingly heretical statement, "Customers don't buy solutions." He credits Bill Stinnett's book, *Think Like Your Customer* (New York: McGraw-Hill, 2004), for influencing many of his ideas about buying. Says Stu, "Consider what customers typically have to go through to make a purchase. They have to research products and vendors, talk to sales reps, figure out the best product or service, get references, sell the idea internally, get management and budget approval, go to purchasing to get a purchase order and possibly legal to review a contract. The only reason a customer does this is to achieve business results." Therefore, Stu says, "Customers don't buy solutions in and of themselves, they buy business results." The solution is the means to the end. "Sales reps love to talk about their solutions. But we should be talking a lot less about our solution and more about the customer's quantifiable, financially viable business results," cautions Stu. He encourages his reps to think like business executives and find ways to help customers find a place on their income statements for the products the reps are offering. Ultimately, that translates to creating value for an organization's shareholders or investors, which is the main objective of every business.

Stu outlines six key questions, again from Stinnett's book, that must be answered in order for a customer to buy (Table 13.1). They are an integral part of the WebEx sales process.

TABLE 13.1   Six Key Customer Questions

1. What is the customer's real business motive or reason for buying?
2. What is the urgency; is there an impending event?
3. What is the impact, payback, or results they expect to achieve?
4. What are the consequences of doing nothing?
5. What resources or means are available?
6. What is the risk associated with making a decision?

RETHINKING THE SALES FUNNEL: STATIC VERSUS DYNAMIC MEASUREMENT

Another revolutionary Sales 2.0 concept that Stu has introduced to WebEx is the idea of dynamic measurement, which he claims is key to their competitive advantage and astounding sales success. Stu challenges his employees to rethink the sales funnel—or universe of potential buyers—and set metrics in terms of funnel shape and velocity rather than quantity of contents. "The most important things to measure are movement and change," states Stu.

Stu explains, "Traditional sales managers are measuring the wrong things when they look at a weekly sales pipeline and forecast. First of all, they measure things like results against quota, average selling price, cost of sales, and gross margin. The problem is these are all trailing indicators that are calculated after the fact when the quarter or year has already closed and you can't do anything about it. What we need instead are leading indicators like lead conversion rates and pipeline multiples. But even if we know, for example, that it takes 100 leads to get to one deal or the pipeline is four times my quota, we're still looking at this information the wrong way. First of all, we're looking at it from a trailing indicator perspective. Second, we need a lot more granularity." See Figure 13.3 for an example of a WebEx sales pipeline report.

Stu poses a challenging question, "What if the value of my pipeline is four times my quota but the deals haven't moved in 90 days? Is it likely the quarterly quota will be met?" Standard questions—such as, "How many opportunities are in my funnel? What is their value? Is the value three or four times my quota?"—Stu explains, "Do not provide any information on which deals were lost, increased or decreased, or moved into the next

The Way It Should Be

…	A	CallOut	Discovery	Solution	Agreement	Contract	Implement
Count	11975	7059	4122	2598	1807	1362	1185
Close Rates From (AB, Prev. Stage)	N/A	58.95%, 58.95%	34.42%, 58.39%	21.70%, 63.03%	15.09%, 69.55%	11.37%, 75.37%	9.90%, 87.00%
Days to Reach	N/A	5.69	7.90	9.77	11.11	13.10	13.92
Days Spent in Stage	5.69	2.21	1.87	1.34	1.99	0.82	N/A

WebEx Sales Pipeline

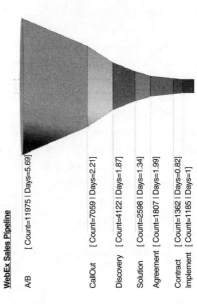

A/B   [Count=11975 | Days=5.69]

CallOut   [Count=7059 | Days=2.21]

Discovery [Count=4122 | Days=1.87]

Solution   [Count=2598 | Days=1.34]

Agreement [Count=1807 | Days=1.99]

Contract   [Count=1362 | Days=0.82]
Implement [Count=1185 | Days=1]

Figure 13.3 WebEx Sales Pipeline Report

quarter. Without this information, pipeline predictability is impossible. This view of the funnel is just a static snapshot that requires having conversations with each sales rep to delve into the specifics of each deal."

WebEx sales managers examine the following when looking at fore-cast reports:

☐   How many new opportunities are there?
☐   What moved up or down in value?
☐   What moved up in stage?
☐   How long did it take to move?
☐   Was the close date moved forward or backward?

By looking at movement and change, sales managers can easily tell at what stages of the sales cycle their deals typically stall, and can delve into the reasons why. Stu suggests starting with a look at the stage prior to the stall. "Chances are something was missed, like getting answers to the six key questions such as a customer's motive, urgency, or available resources," he says.

"After defining your sales process, rethinking the sales funnel in terms of shape and velocity is important because you want to be able to continually and dynamically improve your process, shorten your sales cycle length, reduce the amount of time and effort it takes to close a deal, and win more deals. These are the productivity gains that we see in Sales 2.0," says Stu.

He shows us pictures of two kinds of funnels, and asks questions on how to think about them (see Figure 13.4). These funnels may seem to represent the exact same sales cycle length and lead-to-close (stages 1 to 7) conversion ratio. However, the funnel on the left shows better conversion rates, or movement, from one stage to the next. This funnel is preferable because it shows that opportunities are being qualified out of the funnel early to allow sales reps to focus their time and efforts on deals that are more likely to close. The funnel on the right is not only more costly but could easily result in a severe capacity problem. "A 10 percent improvement in conversion rates in the first two steps of the sales cycle," says Stu, "can result in a 40 percent improvement in sales productivity."

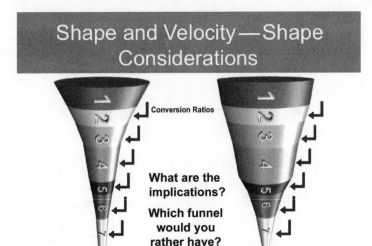

Figure 13.4   Shape and Velocity of the Funnel

As for velocity, or reducing sales cycle length, Stu continues, "The greatest driver to lengthening a sales cycle is not the time it takes to conduct a meeting—it's how long it takes to schedule the *next* meeting. A 10 percent reduction in sales cycle length can increase productivity by 25 percent and move deals into this quarter."

Stu emphasizes the effect of web-touch selling on conversion rates and velocity. "Using web-touch selling, we apply less expensive resources to the early part of the sales cycle, do a better job of qualification, and reach far more prospects per day than with a field sales–only approach," he explains. "Furthermore, with web-touch selling, we are able to access internal resources or experts as well as the customer's decision makers more easily, resolving issues that could get in the way of closing deals quickly."

Getting the WebEx salesforce to adopt the sales process along with the new way of forecasting didn't happen overnight; it took close to two years to implement and fine-tune this process. "The key to the successful transition," Stu informs us, "was getting the first-line sales managers to buy in and reinforce it with their teams without reverting to the comfortable old ways. It took nine months of coaching to get them to change their behavior."

TECHNOLOGY EMPOWERS
THE SALESFORCE

Because he runs WebEx's consulting business, Stu is in a great position to constantly test new ideas in his own organization's sales group. When he can prove their effectiveness in improving sales results in solutions sales, they are rolled out to the rest of the WebEx sales organization. To that end, Stu champions the incorporation of new processes and tools as well as technologies that enable sales processes. But he clarifies that "Sales 2.0 is not about the technology, but rather how the technology empowers the salesforce to achieve unprecedented results."

One of the technologies that Stu introduced to his sales group—which does 90 percent of their deals by Web and phone—is a visual mapping tool called MindManager from Mindjet, which is used in conjunction with a WebEx meeting. By using Mindjet's MindMaps in the discovery or first contact stage, he found that he was able to engage the customer at a much deeper level, resulting in more deals closing faster. Stu built templates of qualification questions for different types of buyers that are preloaded into the system to assist the sales rep and the customer during an initial qualification call. Sales reps ask prospects, "Do you mind if I take notes?" No one ever says "no." Seeing the questions and sales reps' answers on their screens in real time encourages customers to become more interactive as their business challenges, technical environment, and decision process are being discussed. Customers receive immediate confirmation that the rep is listening and understanding their business needs and objectives. If there are misunderstandings or misinterpretations, they can be corrected instantly, which leads to trust in the relationship. The MindMap is then integrated into prospect records and becomes a valuable and "living" reference tool for anyone at WebEx—in sales, support, consulting, or other departments—who has contact with that customer. Stu is also a big fan of using IM (Instant Messenger) for further engagement, and advocates putting prospects and customers on your buddy list. "Why not make it easy for your customers to access you and ask questions when they come up?" he asks.

The solutions sales group also uses software called Landslide that addresses day-to-day productivity. Landslide is a "sales workstyle management" product that takes a process-centric rather than a data-centric approach to automating the salesforce. Its emphasis is on improving the productivity of each individual member of the salesforce. It also produces the kind of pipeline reports that Stu advocates, those that measure movement and change from one sales stage to the next.

As head of WebEx's Solutions Sales, or consulting business, Stu also works with the WebEx client base to improve their sales results using Sales 2.0 sales practices, enabled by WebEx's products. A common objection he hears from his clients' sales reps when emphasizing the importance of tracking and measuring is the response, "Do you want me to sell or fill out forms?" He sees a problem with most companies' ineffective attempts to use technology, which end up making sales reps less productive rather than more. He tells us, "One of our customers was asking their reps to fill out three to four online screens and about 100 fields of data per account. Given how much the reps hated entering data into their CRM system, 95 percent of the fields were being filled out less than 2 percent of time." Stu suggests to sales managers, "You only really need six fields to manage your business." They are:

1. Sales rep's name
2. Account name
3. Opportunity name
4. Deal value
5. Expected close date
6. Sales process stage

"The innovation here is tracking the sales process stage. That's the only one that's going to change on a regular basis. With this minimal amount of data, you can manage the world."

TRANSFORMING A SALES ORGANIZATION TO INCORPORATE SALES 2.0

Another challenge that arises often in Stu's consulting practice with WebEx clients is the question of how to transition them from a high-touch-only salesforce to one using web-touch selling practices. He emphasizes, "You don't go to an organization and tell them they've got to turn their entire field organization into a web-touch selling force tomorrow. That doesn't work." He starts by helping the client define the sales process steps for their particular business as well as the buying steps that their typical client takes. Depending on the business, its market, and customers, there could even be *multiple* sales processes. Then he asks, "Where in your process can we best leverage certain technologies that Web 2.0 makes possible?" Stu believes that the early sales process stages are the ones that lend themselves most easily to a web-touch approach. "For an organization that has always sold face-to-face and is adding an Inside Sales capability, this is a good way to get started," he advises.

WebEx's client Coremetrics, an enterprise software and services company that also sells software as a service, is a good example of an organization that implemented a hybrid model that includes both face-to-face and virtual selling by phone and Web. Online businesses use Coremetrics' software-as-a-service (SaaS) solution to optimize online marketing. Vice President of Worldwide Sales, Jeff Schmidt, says, "Inside or web-touch sales should not be limited to one organization, in my view. We have both territory-based field reps and centralized SMB reps, and the key to my organization's success is making everyone sell as productively and inexpensively as possible while meeting the customers' needs. That means even the traditional enterprise field reps use the phone and Web as much as possible." Taking this approach, implementing a sales process similar to WebEx's with the help of Stu's consulting group, and having strict management focus and discipline, Jeff realized a 40 percent improvement in bookings per rep.

MAKING TELEPHONE/WEB SALES CALLS VISUAL

Stu is a master at generating ideas, and he is constantly looking for ways to do things better. He has been studying the difference in effectiveness between a phone call and a face-to-face meeting in creating trust in human relationships. According to the research he's seen, a phone call alone—without visuals—is only 15 percent as effective as an in-person meeting. The WebEx product suite gives you the added benefit of sharing information on a computer screen, but the live, personal touch of a face-to-face call is still missing. "This," claims Stu, "can easily be addressed by adding a video camera to your workplace." He tells us a story of working with a recent client who told Stu that during their last web-touch call—which had not included video—she felt they had had a good conversation and Stu really understood her business needs. But on their next call, which included video, she exclaimed, "Now I feel I really know you!" and went forward with a consulting engagement. We shouldn't underestimate the value of adding our faces to our sales calls.

Stu is excited about the future of remote sales calls and meetings, given exponential technology improvements. With products like WebEx LiveStream, which brings a perfectly synchronized, TV-quality, high-definition audio/video experience to web meetings, he'll surely be measuring how they accelerate sales results and create process improvements.

Sources in addition to interviews: Podcasts: *www.podtech.net/home/index.php?s=Stu+Schmidt/*; Webinars: *www.webex.com/web-seminars/recorded?Prog=1/*; Transcripts and Videos: *www.sales20conf.com/post_conference_07.htmlInterviews/*.

14
GENIUS.COM: AN EMERGING SALES 2.0 PIONEER

You can tell a lot about companies and their cultures when you walk into their offices. In the entryway of the headquarters for venture-funded start-up, Genius.com Inc. stands an ornate and impressively-sized gong. Upon commenting to the receptionist that this must be a treasured part of someone's Asian art collection, we are told that it has a very special purpose that is employed daily: it is sounded by a sales representative every time a new customer is acquired.

Genius.com is a prime example of a company that is driven by a sales culture so strong that even the engineers who develop the product like to drop by salespeople's desks to hear about what's happening with customers. Marketing Vice President Felicity Wohltman has worked at numerous well-known technology companies and says that she has never in her career worked as closely with a sales team as she does at Genius. Everything her group does is in support of the salesforce. Lead generation is Felicity's primary objective.

DIRECT-RESPONSE MARKETING AND SALES 2.0

In Sales 1.0, direct-response marketing requires months of advance planning. Marketing has to think ahead at least one full quarter to create a promotional piece, have it printed, and then mail hundreds or thousands of letters, postcards, or mailers. They then have to hope that their offer or call to action is strong enough to cause an ample number of qualified buyers to request more information, so that they can justify the cost of the piece plus postage. With the proliferation and acceptance of e-mail communication in business, e-mail marketing—delivering marketing messages and offers using the Internet—has become the medium of choice for many companies, given its clear benefits: immediate delivery and lower cost. With e-mail, campaigns can be developed in days rather than months, and can be implemented with more frequency. But while e-mail marketing allows a marketing group to manage its budget more easily, it also has its challenges. Marketers can send out hundreds or thousands of e-mails, never knowing which prospects even opened a message before deleting it, thereby making it impossible to set appropriate priorities for follow up by sales.

Genius.com, however, has eliminated this uncertainty with its on-demand solution, SalesGenius®. Sales reps using SalesGenius are alerted immediately and in real time using an Instant Messenger (IM)–like tool called the Genius Tracker™—not only when prospects open an e-mail message, but also when someone clicks on a link to their web site. A rep can thus make a phone call at the moment that a prospect is viewing the site. Reps can also determine what web pages are looked at and for how long, which gives them insight into what interests their prospective customers most. With SalesGenius, prospects that are most likely to have a need for the product essentially become self-qualifying. At Genius.com, the salesforce follows up with every prospect that opens the marketing-generated e-mail and clicks on the link to their web site. If sales reps know their prospects are looking at their web site, they are able to initiate a timely follow-up and take days or weeks off the sales cycle while simultaneously meeting the immediate needs of the buyer. Given today's challenge of reaching qualified prospects live rather than via endless voice mails, a rep using SalesGenius has major time-management and priority-setting advantages that can significantly shorten the sales cycle. Considering the power of its SalesGenius solution, it's easy to understand why the Genius team is focused on direct-response e-mail marketing to generate demand.

In Sales 2.0, marketing and sales are part and parcel of the same process: engaging prospects and turning them into customers. At Genius.com, marketing begins the sales process through its weekly lead generation programs. "Everything we do," notes Felicity, "drives customer traffic to our web site; whether it's banner ads such as Yahoo! or Google AdWords, e-mail newsletters, or e-mail blasts using our own or third-party opt-in lists with a call to action." A call to action is an incentive that motivates the prospect to do something, in this case, visit the Genius.com web site. If prospects see enough value, they will react and become engaged. Genius uses a variety of calls to action: invitations to online seminars (webinars) or daily demos, offers for free white papers (topical reports), or booklets (e.g., *Sales 2.0 for Dummies*).

ANALYTICS PROVIDE SALES CYCLE DETAILS

Tracking and measurement are cornerstones of Sales 2.0, and are built into the Genius process. "Different people respond to different calls to action, and we are constantly working with the sales organization to evaluate every single sales campaign that we carry out," says Felicity. Genius uses both salesforce.com and a web analytics package to track and measure results that include response rates, visits to their web site, and cost per click. They closely monitor conversions or changes in status; for example, from opportunity or unqualified lead to qualified lead, or from trial customer to customer. Felicity explains, "We're always evaluating our marketing programs based on these results." This intense focus on metrics is paying off. The current monthly qualified lead volume at Genius is in the thousands and growing, as they better understand which programs interest the most customers and yield the best responses. Their current lead-to-qualified-lead conversion rate is strong, and their average sales cycle is short by industry standards. Hundreds of new trial customers sign up each day. Sales are measured in terms of daily, not monthly or quarterly, results. At Genius, they know their target numbers and exactly what they need to do to achieve them.

At Genius, a turning point in the sales cycle occurs when someone agrees to attend a daily demo or signs up for a trial. Felicity explains, "A major objective for us is to get prospects to try out our product through our trial program. Once someone gets to our web site, our goal is to engage them sufficiently so that they'll click on the "free trial" button. Our product is new enough in concept that people need to experience it to really understand what it can do. When they agree to a trial, assuming they meet the criteria we've established, they become a qualified lead." This is where sales comes in. While marketing continues to communicate to unqualified leads in an effort to engage them further and convert them to qualified leads, sales engages only those leads deemed qualified. In this sense, marketing is acting as a first-line lead qualification function for Inside Sales.

A PROCESS-ORIENTED VP OF SALES

Felicity maintains that Genius's strength in process and discipline, which VP of Corporate Sales Jean Tali brought to the company, makes the trial program work. Jean came to Genius with many years of experience running Inside Sales groups, most recently at PlaceWare and Microsoft, so to her, it is second nature to run a process-driven sales organization. While many companies offer trials, only Sales 2.0 companies have a specific, managed, and effective approach to converting trial customers to full-fledged users. At Genius, it starts with the sales rep following up within twenty-four hours of initial contact to answer questions and walk the prospect through the trial. This includes understanding the customers' business needs, communications preferences, and buying process. Without follow-up, prospects can get busy and often don't make the time to fully utilize the product, or realize how it can help them achieve results in their companies. Says Felicity, "They want to know in five words or less how to get started."

Jean's philosophy on the Genius sales process is that it's a framework, with a beginning, middle, and end. But within that framework, there is flexibility, or "moving joints," as she puts it. She believes following a system too stringently can be detrimental, especially in a young company that is still learning about the best way to communicate with its customers. Instead, she asks her team to focus on key milestones in the sales process, and invites them to experiment with what works best in moving from one milestone to the next. As in other Sales 2.0 environments, sharing good ideas and best practices is common among her reps. Shortening the sales cycle is a common goal. But forcing a rigid process on the customer is not the way to achieve this.

Jean has experienced her share of the sales process gone awry when the customer's buying and communications preferences are not considered. She gives us a precise example of this by describing a recent interaction she had when researching pricing for a well-known product. As a former customer of the product, she is highly educated on its uses and, as many customers do nowadays, went to the company's web site looking for information. Once she was on the web site, a chat window appeared with the question, "How may I help you?" Her answer was, "I'm looking for pricing information. How much does a subscription cost?" At this point, the company's inflexible sales process took over. Rather than giving Jean a simple answer or asking her questions related to her pricing question, the person on the other end of the chat session took her through a standard lead qualification script: "What is your name and title? What company are you with? What state are you in?" Jean played along, thinking, "This could be captured more easily in a phone call," but typing in all the required information. She was then told, "Let me connect you to the person you should talk to." She waited as her chat window changed a few different colors and then saw the new chat message, "Hi, I'm Scott. How can I help you?" Jean responded, "I'm looking for pricing information." And the qualification script started from the beginning! At some point, after Jean had typed about thirty lines of chat, Scott suggested they talk on the phone. Jean felt like she was in a Monty Python skit. She practically had her credit card out, ready to order, and what should have been a five-minute sales transaction became a comedy of errors.

SALES 2.0: EMPOWERING SALES REPS AND CUSTOMERS ALIKE

Contrary to her own experience with this particular company, Jean explains, "In Sales 2.0, it's all about empowering the sales reps: enabling them to do more on their own to assist customers." Although technology is a big help, this process starts with a lean, mean, fully accountable sales team. Jean compares her group to the sales organizations of old that included many more specialized groups such as lead qualifiers, appointment setters, subject-matter experts (typically systems engineers in technology companies), and contracts specialists. At Genius, all those functions have been condensed into one multitalented and flexible salesperson. So rather than having to refer a customer to a technical expert for technical questions or a contracts administrator for agreement concerns, the sales rep addresses the customer's questions across a broad range of topics on the spot and when needed. Jean calls this "just-in-time selling." She suggests that this disappearing segmentation of functions—wherein one sales rep can handle a myriad of customer concerns and requirements—is a trademark of Sales 2.0. For Genius, this method is something of a cost-saving necessity. It is a start-up company where budgets and head count are carefully scrutinized. But there is no doubt that without technology, this one-stop shopping approach would not be possible. For example, without WebEx, Genius sales reps could not do a product demo on the fly while on the phone with a customer. Without SalesGenius performing part of the role of a sales development team, sales reps could not automatically identify interested prospects. And without EchoSign, a web-based signature automation service, reps could not quickly execute a contract or licensing agreement within their salesforce.com application with just the click of a button.

Sales reps aren't the only ones who have been empowered through Sales 2.0 technology; customers have been, too. Online resources like web sites, social networks, wikis, and blogs make product and company information instantly available to prospective buyers. "Furthermore," says Jean, "people buy differently, and in many companies, buying has been decentralized. Customers still have purchasing departments, but many decisions for purchases have been given back to business decision makers. In our case, sales managers no longer have to go through a whole controlled buying cycle like they used to. They still have to get a purchase order approved, but they have been empowered to make the business decision." Therefore, companies can't become Sales 2.0 companies just by implementing advanced sales process and technology. They also need an understanding of how different each customer's buying process is in order to retool and apply sales processes and technology that complement and support each customer's preferred method of buying.

The efficiency benefits of Sales 2.0 for sales reps, their companies, and their customers are clear: everyone's needs are met sooner, or "just in time," as Jean suggests. She claims that "information is exchanged instantaneously at the moment that makes sense." Customers get instant gratification; there are no delays. Ultimately, just-in-time selling shortens the buying cycle as well as the sales cycle, which, Jean tells us, "leads to predictability in sales."

RETHINKING SALES MODELS TO ENGAGE NEW MARKETS

Jean continues, "Many companies that have been selling to large, enterprise accounts are trying to grow by addressing new markets like small and medium-size businesses (SMB). These SMBs buy best-of-breed products, not necessarily a whole product suite of end-to-end solutions from one vendor. So larger companies are trying to figure out how to repackage their products, typically with lower price points, to appeal to these new markets." But changing a product offering is not enough. Jean stresses the importance of rethinking sales strategy. "The question of how to sell to SMB is equally important. We're talking volumes and volumes of prospects, not 5, 10, or 20 major accounts. You can't sell to SMB the same way you sell to large enterprise customers, and most companies haven't figured out how to change how they sell. You need a relatively small number of salespeople who can manage enormous volume in real time. At Genius, we talk about the importance of the three Vs in selling to SMB: volume, velocity, and value. Getting all three right requires a radically different sales method from what most companies have been doing for decades."

To this end, Genius CEO David Thompson blogged about a conversation he had with best-selling author and advisory board member Geoffrey Moore about which businesses benefit the most from a Sales 2.0

approach. David wrote, "[Geoff and I] came at this question from very different perspectives. Geoff is very engaged these days with helping larger companies implement strategies for penetrating the 'long tail' of smaller and medium-size businesses. For years, companies and investors viewed going after this market as 'unrealistic,' and 'too expensive.' The need to crack the SMB code by larger companies, however, has become even more intense as the enterprise software market has become increasingly saturated. These companies are forced to compete with the on-demand software vendors' visionary promise of lower pricing and easier implementation. Note how companies like Oracle and SAP now have full-bore initiatives in the on-demand space."

SALES 2.0 AND CULTURE SHIFT AT GENIUS'S CUSTOMER, BT

BT, the British telecommunications giant, is one of Genius's customers and a wonderful example of a large company making such a transition. Faced with deregulation in its industry and growing competition, BT is motivated to reinvent itself by way of changing its products, markets, and corresponding sales strategies. The initiative to change is coming from the top—which is a requirement for a massive cultural shift of this type—but is also enthusiastically embraced by sales reps. Volumes of SMBs that represent the biggest growth opportunity in decades are increasingly important to BT. BT's business retail arm is looking to Genius to help them market to the mid-market sector by using SalesGenius and a new approach to selling.

However, there can be major challenges in implementing Sales 2.0 practices within large companies that have always sold using more traditional methods. Changing company culture and behavior can take a long time. People are still the most important element of buying and selling, and people are reluctant to accept change, especially if they've been successful all their lives doing something in a certain way. All the process and technology in the world are useless without people to follow and use it. But technology, Jean Tali suggests, can be a conduit to change within a sales organization. Because a wide variety of sales enabling tools are available for the first time, people are starting to ask how they can use them and make their sales organizations more efficient and effective.

HIRING SALES 2.0 REPS

Even Genius, a start-up that launched with a Sales 2.0 strategy from the beginning, has faced implementation challenges. In order to double her sales team every six months, Jean needed to nail her hiring profile and interviewing process. She made mistakes early on identifying the right talent for her full-service sales team. She hired people who fared well in initial interviews, but faltered when on the phone with customers. So Jean asked herself, "What went wrong? What do we need to do differently? How did we not catch this?" and came up with an interviewing process that weeded out clearly unqualified people. She looks for sales candidates with two to three years' selling experience, a passion for learning, and a high degree of self-motivation. But that's not enough. Jean has learned from experience that the Genius environment needs people who, from day one, can comfortably employ the variety of sales enabling tools used in her established sales process. If she worked at a large company with a full-time trainer, she might have the luxury of hiring people without these specific experiences. But she doesn't have time to train; her sales reps must learn the Genius product line on their own time and on the job. And if they don't already have experience with sales technologies like CRM and web conferencing, then they aren't a good fit for Genius right now. There simply isn't time for potential reps to get up to speed on those basics, given how steep the product and industry learning curve is in the beginning, and how many prospects there are. With new product releases coming out regularly—one of the common attributes of on-demand software—product documentation can't be produced fast enough.

The reps that Jean had mistakenly hired had convinced her that they knew how to use the required sales tools; they were salespeople, after all. But once they were on board and it came time to communicate with customers, they simply couldn't utilize the products. Genius sales candidates who make it through an initial screening are now required to make a brief online presentation on a subject of their choosing to the executive team. It can be about anything except for the product that they currently sell. Surprisingly, the candidates that perform the best are not necessarily those that are the most impressive in person. But given the requirements of the job—ease and proficiency with online and phone communication—it was important for Jean to come up with a way to witness someone's skills in context. During the candidates' presentations, it is easy to determine how well they will function within the Genius sales environment with Genius prospects. Jean is able to ask herself: Did they organize the meeting using technology such as an Outlook calendar invitation? How motivated and passionate are they? How well do they use web conferencing? How compelling are they to listen to? How good are their presentation slides? Can they field questions over the phone? Do they close at the end? And perhaps most important, how creative are they?

In addition to sales orientation, creativity and a fun-loving nature are other important characteristics in the culture at Genius. Just look at the example of CEO David Thompson, who sings opera at company holiday parties and coauthored a humorous take on the subject of Sales 2.0 in his brainchild, *Sales 2.0 for Dummies*. Or consider the story of one sales candidate, now a Genius employee, who did a presentation on the topic of his family cat. He explained, using bar charts, how he learned everything about sales from his cat, a great hunter who captures a certain number of birds per year every year.

This candidate was on to something with this story of his cat. Hunters and farmers are important concepts in the Genius sales department. Hunters seek out new customers, while farmers look after customers once they sign up by helping them set up training and get their accounts connected and password-protected. Farmers ensure that the customers have an easy time getting started with the product and have a pleasant and productive experience. While farmers are multitasking, organized relationship-builders, hunters have more of a single-minded focus. Because she believes hunters and farmers have very different skills, Jean allowed for this one specialization and distinction of roles within her sales organization. "A hunter is fantastic at the initial stages of converting a qualified prospect into a customer, but would be lousy at meeting the customer's needs once the initial deal is closed. Farmers, by nature of being more customer-service oriented, will do a better job of keeping customers happy, thereby selling additional products and services within an existing account," she states. David calls her approach "land and expand."

Jean assigns quarterly quotas to both groups, so she can adjust the numbers as the company and its product offerings grow and sales productivity increases. The current assignment per rep is hundreds of thousands of dollars per quarter. About 50 percent of deals come from inbound marketing campaigns and 50 percent come from cold calling by her reps. Jean's metrics management is so sophisticated that she knows not only the optimal activity levels required to make quota but also the percentage of forecasted accounts in different-sized companies. Larger companies have more complex buying processes, so they have longer sales cycles.

Jean also tracks performance differences between new and experienced reps. Reps who have been on board for at least four months produce almost 40 percent more in revenue than new reps. During the four-month period that it takes for new reps to achieve full productivity, Jean watches the metrics carefully to determine who is on track and who may have performance problems. If activity levels and conversion rates don't improve from month two to month three, a situation Jean calls "flatlining," she can predict that in month four, they won't be at quota.

PHONE AND WEB SELLING

Practically every Genius deal is completed by phone and Web, although sales reps can visit customers if absolutely necessary to the customer and if the deal size justifies it. Many of Jean's reps have both inside and outside sales experience. Those with field-selling experience are often tired of the travel required for in-person selling. Their perspective is that if the compensation plan allows them to make enough money, they'd rather use the phone and Web to talk to prospects and stay home at night. Jean has structured a very lucrative compensation plan to meet that need, allowing reps to make double or more their base or guaranteed income in commissions. She believes that high-risk, high-reward plans keep people hungry and producing.

Genius.com exemplifies the notion that a start-up can appear larger than life and achieve greatness with the right amount of passion and progressive methods. This company with fewer than one hundred employees organized and hosted the first Sales 2.0 conference in San Francisco in October 2007. Inspired by Geoffrey Moore, CEO David Thompson led his young but mighty company to make this inaugural event a reality and bring nearly a thousand sales professionals together to discuss the new concept of Sales 2.0. It's part of Genius's mission to teach organizations about innovative sales methods and help them move into the Sales 2.0 world, ideally by using Genius's cutting-edge and proven-successful technology.

15

SYNERON: VISIONARY SALES LEADERSHIP IN AN UNEXPECTED INDUSTRY

Syneron

C EO of Syneron Doron Gerstel was initially concerned about revealing the details of his innovative sales model. "I hope my competitors don't read this book," he pondered. "I consider our nontraditional sales strategy a major competitive edge." He got comfortable within seconds, though, realizing that he still had a unique advantage. The key prerequisites for evolving an existing sales organization into one that successfully engenders Sales 2.0 philosophies and strategies are executive support, willingness to change, and disciplined execution. While Syneron displays these organizational attributes, most businesses the company competes against do not possess all the ingredients necessary to succeed.

Doron, the former president and CEO of Zend Technologies, is the epitome of the creative, visionary risk-taker, a phrase that describes many a technology company leader. He now leads Syneron (NASDAQ: ELOS), a $141 million (FY2007) company that develops and markets aesthetics, which are medical devices that allow physicians to offer noninvasive services such as hair removal, wrinkle and cellulite reduction, and skin rejuvenation. Syneron's proprietary technology, "ELOS," differentiates its products from competitive devices used for laser treatments. But superior technology alone does not guarantee success in the marketplace.

IMPROVING ON THE TRADITIONAL SALES MODEL

The expected and traditional sales approach in the health-care industry is high touch and high cost. For many decades, doctors and their staffs have been personally visited, wined and dined, and invited to enjoy resort vacations in exchange for listening to vendor pitches from sales professionals. The perception has been that, though expensive, these kinds of investments are required to be a contender in the world of medical products.

Doron suspected that this sales model could use improvements in profitability and productivity. "Having reengineered sales at my last company, I believed implementing Inside Sales operations at Syneron would transform the way we do business and have a major impact on our results," said Doron. "But I had to test it first with my customers." To fast-track the project, avoid potentially costly mistakes, and validate new sales concepts in his market, Doron knew to work with trusted and experienced sales experts who think outside of the box. For help designing and executing his Sales 2.0 vision—as well as validating the benefits of a new model—he engaged a sales consulting and executive coaching firm he knew, Unlimited Results, who in turn partnered with Anneke's company, Phone Works, a known leader in innovative sales practices and sales strategy and implementation consulting. Doron's ultimate goals were to decrease the cost of sales, increase revenues, and improve sales productivity. To that end, Doron and the consulting team set about developing a highly profitable, repeatable, scalable sales operation by introducing an Inside Sales function to the existing sales model.

TAKING AN INCREMENTAL APPROACH

Doron had big, expansive ideas for change, but he knew from experience that behavior modification of the way people do business—for both buying and selling—couldn't be accomplished overnight. Too much change too quickly can be disruptive and threatening, and Doron needed to avoid revenue and profit shortfalls. He worked with his consulting team to implement incremental modifications to Syneron's sales approach that would have maximum benefit, while keeping much of the fundamental sales strategy intact. With the intent of testing, validating, and refining the new sales model over the course of the rollout, the consultants took a systematic, four-phase approach to the project. Progression from each phase to the next depended on achieving positive outcomes and results in the previous phase. Phase 1 commenced with a jump-start project plan that followed Phone Works's tested and proven methodology for starting Inside Sales groups from scratch. The consultants started with an analysis of Syneron's specific business, market, and customers, which included interviewing and sharing ideas with over 30 of Syneron's executive managers, field sales regional and territory managers, marketing communications and product marketing specialists, as well as physician and nurse customers. The Phase 1 deliverable included an Inside Sales strategy recommendation uniquely tailored to Syneron's business, and corresponding implementation plan and time line. Before proceeding with the execution of the plan, these recommendations were presented to Doron for acceptance and approval.

The proposed strategy and implementation plan recommendations centered on the following:

☐   Restructuring sales to create a newly established Inside Sales group with distinct roles and responsibilities for different sales cycle steps.

☐   Articulating well-defined, consistent sales processes mapped to Syneron's different buyer segments.

☐   Developing revenue and activity targets with an ROI model to test against.

☐   Defining job descriptions for the new members of the sales organization.

☐   Determining appropriate compensation plan structures for each role.

☐   Designing training programs.

☐   Specifying marketing requirements to support the group.

☐   Outlining needs for sales tools customized for phone-based reps.

☐   Implementing systems to provide closed-loop information on the status of customers and outcomes of activities.

Three distinct Inside Sales functions were specified within the organization: sales development for initial qualification of sales leads, Telesales for sales of warranties and upgrades, and customer care for customer communications before and after the sale and streamlining of the order process.

IMPLEMENTING SALES DEVELOPMENT TO GENERATE AND QUALIFY LEADS

One of Doron's key concerns was the sales productivity of his field sales organization, a group that never seemed to have enough good leads and who consistently sucked the pipeline dry at the end of every quarter. To address this issue, the consultants' Phase 1 plan called for an increase in the quantity of qualified sales opportunities and a decrease in the length of the sales cycle by introducing the concept of a sales development group. Sales development would leverage the existing field sales organization by focusing on the early stages in the sales cycle and by handling the first interactions with a potential buyer. There would be no radical changes in the high-touch field sales approach beyond the initial sales lead generation and qualification; sales development's objective was to set face-to-face appointments between field reps and prospective buyers. But the group would ensure that these visits would only be offered to physicians who were truly interested and qualified to buy Syneron's products. The field reps' requirement to constantly find new sales opportunities while at the same time closing business would also be alleviated by the addition of a group that was dedicated to lead generation and qualification. The corresponding sales efficiency improvements would result in better close rates and increased revenues.

MINING THE CUSTOMER BASE

There was another untouched source of new revenue on the other end of the sales life cycle. A Telesales group—called Inside Sales at Syneron—would generate incremental, untapped revenue from existing customers who didn't regularly hear from Syneron, given the field's focus on closing new business. The consulting team assumed that Syneron customers would be more likely to buy warranties and upgrades without requiring a face-to-face visit, due to their familiarity and experience with the company and its products. With the addition of Telesales, sales productivity gains were expected in the field as well. In the past, field reps were asked to manage existing accounts as well as sell to new ones, which divided their focus. But by providing a lower-cost resource to look after customers, new business *and* customer sales would increase. The client experience would improve, too, thanks to the attention they received from Syneron after their purchase. For companies with a field-sales-dominant Sales 1.0 history, the introduction of a sales development group and a Telesales function for customer accounts is a relatively nondisruptive and proven way to achieve the cost-saving, productivity-enhancing benefits of a Sales 2.0 strategy. Doron's confidence in the plan was boosted by knowing that Phone Works had been doing similar projects for over 250 customers since the early 1990s—and had enjoyed excellent results.

PILOTING THE NEW PROGRAMS

Phase 2 consisted of piloting each of the new Inside Sales programs. These pilots or trials were designed to make sure that this new way of capturing interest and selling medical devices to customers would be accepted by the market and customer base. The pilots would also answer these key questions: Would Syneron's prospective customers object to contacts by more than one member of the Syneron sales team? Would users of Syneron's equipment need to speak to the person who originally sold them their product? Could the company justify the cost of additional sales resources in their customer acquisition and growth strategy? Phase 3—which would be launched only if the pilot results warranted an expansion—was the comprehensive program implementation: getting full-time Syneron sales development and Telesales reps on board and training them; setting up the systems and operations; more fine-tuning of the program and processes; and transitioning the management of the operation to a full-time Syneron senior executive of Inside Sales. Phase 4 focused on optimization and included ongoing management assistance and review for continued assessment of results, and further refinement and revision of the model.

The objective of the sales development pilot was not only to generate new qualified sales opportunities for Syneron's field sales reps, but also to validate a repeatable process for doing so on a consistent and predictable basis. The pilot simultaneously allowed Syneron to discover some important market data by testing messaging, positioning, target markets, common questions and objections, and buyer preferences. When examining a new Inside Sales function through a pilot program, a good idea is to introduce change incrementally until the results are proven. It is common to limit the testing to one or two Inside Sales reps engaging with a subset of a company's market, and it is especially helpful to launch a pilot program in a territory owned by a cooperative field rep or team, who understands the benefits of the new program and won't try to sabotage it. In Syneron's case, one experienced and highly skilled Inside Sales specialist from consulting partner, Phone Works, spent three days a week for 12 weeks contacting a list—procured by Marketing—of over 1,500 doctors located in key cities in a geographic region that mapped to the places where Syneron field sales reps were based. The targeted doctors had been identified as those already providing some kind of aesthetic procedure to their patients. Aaron Ross, founder of salesforce.com's outbound sales development organization, refers to this kind of highly targeted outbound campaign as Cold Calling 2.0.

The consulting team used information gleaned during interviews to evaluate the target markets, solution set, and complexity of the sale, and delivered a nine-step sales process, aligned with the customers' buying process—starting with an "Inquiry/Unqualified Lead" stage and ending with the eighth and ninth stages, "Closed Sale" and "Account Management." To ensure measurement, tracking, and follow-up, Syneron's CRM system—salesforce.com—was set up to capture and report on information gathered by the sales development rep, including a lead ranking indicator of a prospect's readiness to buy (A = Excellent potential, B = Good potential, C = Potential not defined, D = No potential);

a lead source (where the lead came from); time frame for purchase; decision-making criteria; and other data pertinent to a follow-up sales call by a field sales rep. The team also developed sales tools specific to the pilot, including call guides outlining qualification questions relevant to different customer types and consistent sales messages to be tested.

The consultants also set target results according to industry best practices and their understanding of Syneron's business. They built a straw-man model and outlined likely sales process metrics, based on their knowledge of industry standards. They included a ramp-up time of four weeks for training and getting the program off the ground. This included an assumed number of contact attempts per day (calls, e-mails, faxes), an estimated connect rate (the percentage of phone calls resulting in a live conversation with the right person, rather than voicemail), and most importantly, the number of qualified leads that could be delivered to the field. Based on these numbers, the consulting team then modeled expected revenue results, by applying values for average deal size, sales cycle length, and close rate assumptions once the leads were passed to the field.

By developing this kind of model, Sales 2.0 companies can evaluate sales performance against expectations, and adjust accordingly as results are tracked. Companies that launch new programs or products, or manage their businesses without understanding their sales metrics, will find it impossible to make predictions about what is coming from quarter to quarter. They also won't recognize the early warning signals associated with market changes or slowdowns—which can severely damage company value and relationships with investors if adjustments aren't made. The Sales 2.0 approach requires constant tracking and improvement of key metrics to ultimately produce more higher-value customers and predictable results. Table 15.1 shows what the sales development pilot activity model looked like.

The Telesales pilot, the second of two trials, was designed to generate incremental revenue from existing Syneron customers using a lower-cost sales channel than the field. Doron wanted the field focused on finding large new business orders, but he suspected that money was being left on the table in regards to physicians who already had purchased one or more Syneron systems. The consulting team developed a 10-week outreach campaign to existing Syneron customers in two geographic territories whose three-year warranties or leases were due to expire in the next 12 months, as well as those who had not purchased new equipment in six months. A Syneron employee was recruited from another department to play this Telesales and account management role. With the primary objective of renewing the physician's service contract, she would take the in-the-moment opportunity to explore the customer's current business needs and medical practice aspirations, and potentially uncover new sales opportunities for additional Syneron products. While doing this, she would also test and validate the sales and buying process steps, contact and sales conversion rates, offers, and messages that were outlined for this audience by the consultants in the planning stage. A separate set of metrics was developed, based on best-practice estimations from the consultants' previous experiences with similar types of customer revenue programs.

EXCEEDING EXPECTATIONS WHILE GAINING INTELLIGENCE

At the conclusion of Phase 2, both pilots exceeded expectations. The sales development pilot yielded 19 qualified leads for the field in 12 weeks—with a sales development person only working part-time. Of

TABLE 15.1 Sales Development Pilot Metrics

Metrics	Output Assumption
Number of outbound calls and e-mails per day/week/pilot period including ramp	45/135/1521
Contacts (connects, returned calls and returned e-mails) per day/week/month at 12 percent rate	5/15/183
Percent of contacts in A lead category	4 percent
Number of contacts per pilot period in A lead category	7
Percent of contacts in B category	6 percent
Number of contacts per pilot period in B lead category	11
Average deal size	$80,000
Pipeline value per month (A/B leads)	$1.44 million

those 19 opportunities, 2 closed, resulting in $125,000 in same-quarter bookings. However, of the remaining 17 opportunities generated in the pilot, 6 more deals, with a higher average selling price (ASP) of $80,000, were forecast to close in the following quarter. The total value of forecasted deals resulting from the pilot was close to $600,000.

An important discovery was that the ASP for deals closed by the field generated during the pilot was $20,000 less than assumed in the projections. While we had a revenue target during the pilot, it should be noted that we set the revenue expectations conservatively and viewed them as icing on the cake, given our part-time involvement, emphasis on training, ramping up and testing the program, and getting Syneron's sales reps accustomed to working in a new way. As referenced in Part 1, Chapter 5, we were following Leslie and Holloway's advice to observe a Sales Learning Curve before scaling up the program and raising sales quotas. Executives chronically underestimate the amount of time it takes to get new Inside Sales reps up to speed, and they usually overestimate their revenue contributions in their first quarter. Similarly, they often overestimate ASP and underestimate sales cycle length. With the measurement discipline involved in Sales 2.0, these actual numbers finally come to light.

The second pilot—teleselling to customers—generated over $225,000 in incremental revenues in 10 weeks. Of 17 qualified opportunities found, 10 closed at an average order size of over $20,000. At the conclusion of the pilot period, the pipeline value for warranty and lease renewals and new product sales opportunities within the customer base was over $350,000.

In addition to the financial results, there were valuable lessons learned from the pilots. An advantage to being a first mover in Sales 2.0 practices for your market is that it's often a lot easier to reach prospects by phone when none of your competitors are calling them. The sales development pilot yielded contact rates that were more than three times better than the Phone Works best-practices assumptions (based on experience with technology clients), proving that Syneron's decision makers were accessible and would accept communication by telephone. In addition, it took fewer call attempts than estimated to connect and have a conversation with a prospective buyer. It wasn't always possible to get a physician on the phone, but other decision makers in the doctor's office were identified during the course of the project. The team also uncovered important information during their exchanges and engagements with prospects. They reported that certain tested messages were much more effective than others, and that some special offers unexpectedly yielded a very low number of qualified opportunities. There were certain products and services that could easily be sold by telephone, while others required a demo and face-to-face visit. Customers' communications preferences and common objections were uncovered and tracked as well. Unlike buyers in other markets, Syneron's customers—medical professionals—are more accustomed to receiving important information (such as lab reports) via fax than by e-mail, a fact that was revealed during the course of the pilot. Finally, there were important discoveries made—in addition to relative strengths and weaknesses—for each list of prospects tested. For example, some potential clients had characteristics that rendered them immediately unqualified, which could be identified up front before calling. Being aware of these criteria in advance will increase productivity going forward, as calls will not be made to this audience in the future.

By setting targets and modeling expected metrics and results against targets in advance, Syneron began to realize the power of Sales 2.0 practices. The company was no longer shooting in the dark in regards to sales, and had a very clear picture of its pipeline development process, its customers' concerns, its sales process for warranties and add-ons, and how to be effective going forward. Sales 2.0 companies have market intelligence. They align their salesforce with customer opportunities for maximum benefit. They understand their businesses and their buyers better than their competitors. They continually track and measure their process to ensure that it evolves as economic and corporate variables change.

SCALING THE ORGANIZATION

Armed with the assurance he needed that Inside Sales concepts would work for Syneron—*and* complement his existing field sales team—Doron was ready to enter into Phase 3 of the project: to scale up his Inside Sales team after the promising results of the two pilots. "When you have measurable results and can see the before and after pictures, you can be confident that changing the way you sell is worth the investment." Doron again looked to his consultant experts for further clarification and advice before finalizing the headcount and resources budget associated with a sales reorganization. A full ROI model, which showed expected costs and returns associated with the Inside Sales expansion, was developed. The implementation time line, staffing, and rollout plans were refined based on the results shown in the pilots and a realistic feel for what was possible in Syneron's prospect and customer universes. Recommendations such as future marketing campaigns, refined sales process, systems improvements, and sales tools needed were made. A key decision was to go forward immediately with the recruitment of an Inside Sales leader—one who was not only well-versed in Inside Sales process, systems, metrics, and productivity tools, but who also had the rare experience of scaling up a new Inside Sales group. Doron approved the hiring initiatives upon the consultants' delivery of a full cost/benefit analysis, which used informed numbers tested in the pilots.

Syneron also faced some immediate practical questions, which are common for companies starting a new Inside Sales operation: where in the world to put it, and whether to centralize the insides sales reps or decentralize them into each geographic region or territory? As with many businesses these days, Syneron's offices are organized by function with locations worldwide, including Irvine, CA, and Toronto, which serve the North American market. The consultants evaluated the pros and cons of each location, based on cost, availability of resources, and a number of other factors. After weighing the options, the consultants recommended a centralized Toronto-based hub.

These decisions proved fateful for Lynn D'Aoust, Vice President, Toronto Operations, who was recruited to head up the inside team in December 2006. With a background selling and managing Inside Sales organizations for Xerox Canada, Bull HN, Datamirror, and WH Brady, Lynn was the perfect hire to take Syneron to the next level, once the pilot programs showed that the model worked. Xerox's sales training program was considered one of the very best in the 1980s, when Lynn cut her teeth in the industry. "When I met Doron and heard about his vision, approach to implementation, and ultimate goal, I knew I wanted to join the company," says Lynn. She continues, "Numbers speak for themselves, and seeing the results of the pilots, I was confident the program would succeed."

With an implementation plan and his key manager in place, Doron was eager to realize his vision. Fortunately, Lynn was able to ramp her group and produce results very quickly, thanks to the piloting and planning work done by the consultants. Having an implementation plan to follow along with the tested processes defined through the pilot programs really made a difference. By following the process prescribed in the plan and tracking against validated, Syneron-specific metrics and results, Lynn can now predict what sales development will produce and deliver to the field on a consistent quarterly basis. Similarly, by using the plan's training guide, she gets new sales development reps up to full speed in less than two months.

If there was one challenge in meeting Doron's expectations to move forward at light speed, it was Lynn's insistence that they carefully interview and hire the right people. Lynn says adamantly, "Hurry up and hire doesn't work. You can lose a lot of ground with hiring mistakes." Given Syneron's commitment to promoting from within, Lynn looks for relatively young people with university degrees who are starting their careers in sales and are interested in a career path to the field. Sales development reps typically are promoted to either customer care or Telesales before graduating to a field position. From there, a promotion is contingent on a variety of factors: consistent performance, demonstration of sales and product skills, and the opening of a new field territory.

Lynn continued where the pilots left off: with a charter of expanding the new sales development and Telesales functions, as well as fine-tuning customer care. In sales development, Lynn initially focused on hiring three sales development reps—one for each of Syneron's sales regions. She sought out people with experience making highly targeted phone calls to prospective buyers; the group more than doubled in the first year. Using salesforce.com, the group calls contacts on lists purchased from list brokers, as well as personal contacts provided by the field sales reps, who are asked to forward their virtual Rolodexes for loading into the system. While producing qualified leads for immediate follow-up by the field, sales development continues to gather important business intelligence for future campaigns. A buyer who isn't adding an aesthetics practice right away but has plans to do so in six months or a year, for example, is marked accordingly in the system for follow-up at that time. "At the end of each quarter, we used to focus only on closing deals, and every sale that could be made was made. As a result, the field reps were starting the new quarter with zero in the pipeline," Lynn remarked. With the sales development team in place to keep the pipeline consistently full, that doesn't happen anymore.

IMPROVING PRODUCTIVITY AND RESULTS

As her team becomes more experienced and proficient, the numbers keep getting better. Lynn raised her sales development reps' quarterly targets for qualified leads by more than 20 percent in the first year—and the reps keep exceeding their targets. Nine months after they started, the team delivered two and a half times the number of opportunities per rep since their first quarter. As Lynn increased the sales development staff by a factor of two and increased their productivity, the qualified lead volume grew sixfold. In the first quarter, the field responded by winning 11 deals, contributing $1.1 million in sales. Two quarters later, the field rallied to close 72 deals worth $6.7 million in incremental revenue.

How did Lynn manage her team to produce these kinds of expo-nential improvements over the course of the year? "We got better at communicating with our customers. We learned what to say in response to understanding their business needs and concerns." Doctors looking to expand their practices with the purchase of one or more Syneron products are not typically schooled in business, particularly sales and marketing. Syneron makes a concerted effort to help its target audi-ence with medical practice marketing. The company offers not only an online ROI calculator, but also educational forums and free online cus-tomer training that cover topics that can help its customers' bottom lines. Topics include asking for referrals, developing incentive campaigns, and tracking and monitoring advertising.

"We also got better at communicating with the field sales organi-zation, lead qualification and conversion," Lynn continues, explaining her group's increased productivity over time, "and the best results come from the teams that work best together and talk every day." "Sales de-velopment rep to field rep is now 1:3." The field now considers sales development indispensable, and they keep asking for more and more resources. Doron is delighted, too. "The model is working so well that our head of sales is now pushing to increase the number of sales development reps per field rep." The company aims to improve the ratio to 1:2 between sales development and the field.

ADDRESSING CHALLENGES

In the beginning of the rollout, though, it wasn't so easy. Some field reps "didn't get it," Lynn told us. "We were delivering hot opportunities from sales development, and some reps weren't doing anything with them. They didn't use the system, didn't follow up in a timely manner, and the leads got cold." The field needed time to get used to and understand the new process. They also needed to develop trust in the new organization's ability to recognize potential customers and generate qualified leads. Furthermore, some reps weren't that thrilled about the new level of visibility and accountability to which they were being held, given that everything was being tracked in the system. They weren't accustomed to their managers accessing so much information about the timeliness of their follow-ups and their productivity levels in general. Having introduced similar groups at her previous companies, Lynn knew to work closely with the sales managers to answer questions, allay fears, and get the buy-in she needed to make the program work. It helped considerably that she had Doron's full support. And it became clear over time that the regions that had the best collaboration between sales development and the field produced the best sales results and the happiest customers. Today, the group is more than recognized and appreciated by their partners in the field. In fact, two sales development reps received MVP awards in their region at a recent sales kickoff event. The field considers sales development an important ingredient of its ongoing success in a highly competitive industry. And the inside reps have embraced the spirit of competition as well. "Healthy peer competition is key to the organization," Lynn explains. "The reps are eager to outperform their teammates, produce the most qualified leads and achieve the best conversion rates." She encourages this by running sales contests, but insists on quality along with quantity. The reps also feel close to their field rep partners now, even though Inside Sales and the field are geographically dispersed. The sales development team enjoys getting accolades from the field, and strives to be part of a top-performing team.

Telesales has also produced stellar results. "They paid for themselves and then some," says Lynn. This group of three—mapped to Syneron's three field regions—exceeded the plan's expectations. They also increased customers' warranty renewal rates every quarter. Syneron's customers may not experience problems with their purchases for many years, if ever, and in the past, many tended to take the risk that nothing would go wrong with their equipment, and fail to renew their service contracts. But with a salesforce dedicated to selling warranties—a relatively low-priced item for Syneron—over half of Syneron's customers now renew their warranties and the renewal rate has improved 8 percent since the Telesales group's first quarter selling. Having this special sales team also frees the field to focus where they should: on larger new business opportunities, which are imperative for the company's market share growth.

An added benefit of Telesales calling into the customer base is that in addition to uncovering interest in warranty renewal, they have an opportunity to discover new business initiatives that could translate to additional sales opportunities for Syneron. A medical spa looking to add new body contouring services in addition to laser hair removal, for example, would be in the market to evaluate another Syneron product. Supported by some very high-profile public relations—including television appearances on Rachael Ray and Dr. Phil—the reps can introduce new products to customers looking to expand their practices. The news clips are available on Syneron's web site, along with clinical papers for each product line. Telesales reps carry quota for both warranty sales and additional product sales and upgrades. Some of these sales can be made by phone, but some customers still require an on-site demo and are passed to the field to close. To ensure cooperation, both groups are compensated for add-ons while only Telesales is paid commission on warranty renewals.

Velashape is an example of one of Syneron's popular products gaining interest from media, consumers, and physicians interested in offering additional services (Figure 15.1). A device offering thinner thighs definitely grabbed *my* attention! Lynn directed me their web site, where patients can locate their nearest treatment center.

As was the case with sales development, some field reps initially had some issues with Telesales calling into their accounts. Lynn's response was, "They're not a field customer or an Inside Sales customer, they're a

Figure 15.1   This Ad Appeared in Lynn's E-Mails to Me—I Admit It—I Clicked

Syneron customer." The pilot did allow for some holdouts: accounts in which field reps were already forecasting add-on sales when the Inside Sales program began. In the future, savvy field reps will welcome turning over customer deals to Telesales while they work on yet another sale to maximize their income, given the double compensation program.

Lynn's customer care group, also aligned with each sales region, provides sales assistance and customer service and is a liaison between the field, Syneron customers, and other parties involved in purchases. Before a sale, they handle everything from quotes to deal structuring to financing and leasing. They also follow up once a deal is approved to ensure that paperwork is complete, products are shipped and received, and revenue is recognized. When a new customer comes on board, it is the customer care associate who welcomes him to Syneron, provides information, and takes incoming calls when questions arise. With their business practice support model, the reps are eager to help customers succeed with their Syneron products. If a customer's aesthetics business isn't going well, the team is there to provide ideas to help them market the services more effectively.

EXPERIMENTING WITH OUTSOURCING

Like many companies, Syneron experimented with outsourcing Inside Sales services, because of its benefits of increasing resources without increasing staffing. When the field first saw the value of sales development expertly offloading the early sales cycle steps and delivering really great leads, they did what most sales reps do: they asked for more. At that time, though, the staffing budget for sales development had already been spent, so Doron asked Lynn to work with an outside vendor to increase the volume of qualified leads. Though Lynn gave the same exact training to the outsourced sales development group, she did not see the same quality results from her outsource partner as she did with her internal team. "They delivered great quantities of leads, but they just weren't qualified," she said. "I had to turn them over to my own sales development reps to requalify, and that defeated the purpose." After six weeks, she abandoned the project.

ENABLING SALES WITH TECHNOLOGY

As a Sales 2.0 company, Syneron recognizes the enabling power of technology in the sales function. The company is starting to look at additional software tools to enhance sales productivity, but they've wanted to get the basic sales processes right first. "We keep improving our metrics," Lynn says. "We're measuring more and more, and we're trying new things every quarter. Experimentation and measurement are cornerstones of Sales 2.0." Doron concurs. "Sales tools have gotten better in creating transparency and understanding flow," he says. "But though tools are important, the right processes, mindset, and leadership are even more critical. You have to believe that there is a better way of selling and be willing to change."

PART 4

Getting Started with Sales 2.0

HOW CAN SALES 2.0 WORK FOR YOU?

Now you understand what Sales 2.0 is all about, why it is imperative for your company's long-term success, and how Sales 2.0's strategic alignment, sales process, customer relationships, and enabling technology play key roles in your sales productivity improvement. You have learned how companies such as Oracle, WebEx, Genius, and Syneron have implemented Sales 2.0 practices to generate success for their businesses and customers. In our final section, we leave you with some practical ideas on how to get started with this new approach to generating revenue.

But this book can only take you so far. For more information and an ongoing discussion of Sales 2.0 strategy, people, process, and technology, we invite you to stay in touch with us and the Sales 2.0 community on our web site, *www.sales20book.com.* We also provide a Resources Appendix at the back of this book that includes a number of the professional consultants, training professionals, and technology companies mentioned in this book that can help with your evolution from Sales 1.0 to Sales 2.0. We will continue adding to this list of resources on the web site.

We look forward to hearing about *your* experiences with Sales 2.0. In the spirit of Sales 2.0, let's share some best practices and build a community! Go to *www.sales20book.com* and tell us your ideas!

16
YOUR SALES 2.0 PLAN: MAKING A TRANSITION

When considering strategic moves from Sales 1.0 to Sales 2.0, there are some important ideas to keep in mind for your Sales 2.0 plan. In Part 1, we presented the framework of strategy, people, process, and technology and discussed how they differ in Sales 1.0 and Sales 2.0. See Table 3.1 in Chapter 3 for a summary of these differences.

There is no single formula for making you a Sales 2.0 company, however. Only you can determine the priorities that will have the greatest impact on your sales effectiveness and business results and be right for your customers and salespeople.

Whatever initiatives you decide to adopt, consider the most important elements in making a transition from Sales 1.0 to Sales 2.0:

1. *Think differently.* Accept the fact that the future success rate of what you have been doing to get results for years and years is in peril. Be prepared to make difficult changes in culture and mindset. This includes recognizing the power of science and process in the sales function in addition to art, viewing your organization from your customer's point of view, and potentially redefining your sales strategy, people, process, and technology accordingly.

2. *Pilot new initiatives.* Experimentation is an important idea in Sales 2.0. You can't affect culture change with abrupt, sweeping changes. Pilot Sales 2.0 initiatives—whether they involve new strategy, people, process or technology—with a small number of people who are most likely to succeed. Measure their sales performance before and after the pilot program. Don't expect to get it perfect. The pilot is all about testing and experimentation, and you can make changes and fine-tune as you go. Once you make the improvements, you can roll out the program to a larger group. When introducing the new initiative, approach it the same way you would plan a new product launch: with a supporting marketing campaign. Build excitement. Emphasize successes and personal wins. Be creative with a rollout that fits your company culture: have a kickoff event, add a special feature to your internal portal, or develop a fun video featuring internal success stories.

3. *Be patient, and constantly fine-tune.* Changing thinking, let alone behavior, is not easy. The evolution to Sales 2.0 doesn't happen all at once. Give your pilot programs enough time—at least a quarter, preferably longer—to show results. There's no one moment when you suddenly become a Sales 2.0 company. You've read about how WebEx took two years to perfect its advanced sales process and salesforce.com took close to a year to test its Cold Calling 2.0 operation before hiring a full team, and these companies are still looking for ways to improve. Sales 2.0 leaders continuously assess and fine-tune their organizational efficiency, effectiveness with customers, and sales approaches.

With these preconditions in mind, here are some ideas to consider for your Sales 2.0 plan. Think about what makes the most sense for your business; this list is by no means exhaustive:

☐ With Marketing, create or amend your lead ranking system, definition of qualified leads, and the programs to generate them.

☐ Address any alignment issues between Sales and Marketing by revisiting target markets, pricing, positioning, or other topics together.

☐ Identify customers or sales opportunities that can be better and more profitably served by phone and Web; quantify your major opportunity types and align them with the appropriate sales channel.

- ☐ Identify sales cycle steps that can be accomplished effectively without face-to-face meetings.
- ☐ Restructure your sales organization to include Inside Sales groups to take advantage of these opportunities.
- ☐ Revisit your sales hiring profile and interviewing practices: do the reps you're hiring fit into a Sales 2.0 culture, or can they make the transition?
- ☐ Review compensation plans and include bonuses to reward team selling, long-term customer relationship development, and other Sales 2.0 practices.
- ☐ Do an operations review of your sales organization from your customers' point of view. Design or redesign and implement sales processes based on your customers' buying processes.
- ☐ Measure marketing program effectiveness using sales process and technology.
- ☐ Establish your key metrics to track via your sales process, including ASP, average sales cycle length, conversion rates, pipeline and qualified lead volume needed to reach quota, and ramp-up time for new reps. Test and refine these metrics using your sales process.
- ☐ Identify best-performing reps and the process they follow; design a process for sharing their best practices.
- ☐ Pick technology to pilot and measure its effect on your sales team productivity and results.

In the following chapters, we encourage you to think about applying some specific Sales 2.0 initiatives within the framework of strategy, people, process, and technology and give you examples of several companies' approaches.

17

SALES 2.0 STRATEGY: REALIGNING YOUR SALES ORGANIZATION

S ales 2.0 companies align the sales and marketing functions as a prerequisite to increased productivity and results. They also assign the right sales resources to the right opportunity or customer types. One of the ways to transition to Sales 2.0 is to assess your sales team and restructure it to reach more customers, improve engagement, and increase profitability. In Part 2, we introduced the benefits of Inside Sales groups. Think about how sales development and Telesales might work in your company, or if you have Inside Sales groups already, how you can make them more effective. Here's an approach that one company took.

OPTIMIZING THE BALANCE BETWEEN TELESALES AND FIELD RESOURCES

An internal sales effectiveness analysis at Blue Pumpkin Software found that the field salespeople were spending too much time on small to medium-size projects such as product upgrade sales to customers that could have been handled more effectively by a Telesales channel. Meanwhile, more than half of the field salespeople were not making their quotas, and the two Telesales reps were inundated with opportunities. Even worse, customers were not receiving the desired level of service on all transactions. The company was not effectively aligning the sales team with the needs of its buyers. The sales organization had no sales resources to handle those small to medium-size opportunities, leaving the field salespeople with little to no choice when the customer called them directly asking for assistance. As a result of the internal sales effectiveness analysis, Blue Pumpkin increased the size of the Telesales team from two to four people and a Telesales team manager was added. The field salespeople were subsequently able to focus more of their time on larger, more strategic opportunities. The larger Telesales team was able to produce nearly twice as many upgrade sales as before, which had a strategic value beyond the revenue they generated. Since migrating customers to the latest version of the software made them happier, they were less likely to leave for a competitor—a positive outcome on their lifetime value as a customer. The combined, positive results from this relatively simple staffing model change quickly showed up in the forecast and orders report. Within two years, revenue from the Telesales team doubled, and about twice as many field salespeople started exceeding their quotas.

Could you positively affect customer retention rates and satisfaction levels as well as revenue results by reassigning your sales resources?

Witness Systems performed a similar analysis of its customer base and salesforce alignment in 2005. With almost 1,000 customers in North America and approximately 30 field salespeople, the ratio of customers per salesperson was very high. The result of the salesforce alignment analysis was the addition of additional Telesales team members who were chartered with increasing sales to "corporate accounts," or to customers with fewer than 500 users. Because of their relatively small size, corporate accounts often did not receive attention from field sales reps, however, corporate accounts produced significant revenue for the company, and they typically placed add-on orders without a site visit. They also represented a large opportunity for upgrades and new products, although not as large as the most strategic "named" accounts where the field reps spent most of their time and focus. Witness created a Telesales team to serve this customer segment, and results quickly followed. The Telesales team has grown each year since 2005, and has achieved double-digit growth in sales annually to corporate accounts.

For more examples of factors that justify restructuring the sales organization and how they can affect your salespeople and your customers, please visit our book's web site at *www.sales20book.com/resources*.

18

SALES 2.0 PEOPLE: ASSESSING STAFFING, TRAINING, AND COMPENSATION

W ho are the right types of salespeople to effectively implement a Sales 2.0 initiative? They are not necessarily young college grads or technology buffs; rather, the right people are the ones who are most capable of adapting to change. Becoming a Sales 2.0 company requires staffing your organization with the right kinds of salespeople: those who are customer-focused and collaborative and are willing to follow technology-supported processes. There will be times when you will need to implement new sales processes, or make adjustments to the sales model based on new Sales 2.0 initiatives. You will likely introduce new technologies to simplify or automate existing processes. Flexibility and adaptability to change are key attributes for Sales 2.0 success.

Along with your Sales 2.0 staffing initiatives, make sure your training and compensation programs are up-to-date to keep Sales 2.0 reps motivated and producing. Here are some examples of Sales 2.0 initiatives in the "people" category.

UPDATING INTERVIEWING PROCESSES

In addition to optimizing your sales process, improving the processes around hiring and managing your staff is also critical. How do you know which internal or external candidates are the best fit for your Sales 2.0 team? In Phone Works's experiences working with executives who align their businesses with the concepts of Sales 2.0, we find that adjusting hiring processes improves the probability of hiring right the first time. Consider asking interview questions to determine candidates' flexibility, such as their experiences dealing with new technology or process changes in previous positions. Companies hiring Inside Sales candidates or field candidates whose customers may prefer phone and web interactions do not do interviews face-to-face, at least not until candidates have shown their selling capabilities by phone and online. In the Genius.com profile, we describe how web-based presentations are a crucial part of the interview process for prospective sales candidates. In the Sales 2.0 spirit of experimenting with innovative sales practices or piloting new technologies, why not test-drive your sales candidates, too?

USING TOOLS TO PINPOINT HIRING PROFILES

Sales candidate assessment or personality tests such as the ones offered by Caliper, Sales Judge, and Profiles International can provide you with a sales profile for potential employees that can give you additional insight into how they would perform on the job. These assessments are guidelines that can also be used to compare candidates against top performers in the existing sales organization. This process of getting additional insight on a candidate is analogous to performing account research on a customer or prospect before making the next step. Both are processes that leverage technology to reduce risk and increase the likelihood of success.

RETHINKING SALES 2.0 POSITIONS AND RECRUITING

Dave Sterenfeld, a veteran recruiter at Corporate Dynamix, has been filling Silicon Valley sales positions for over 20 years. He reports that there are now more open job requisitions for telesales reps than for field reps. Some companies are even experimenting with hybrid reps, who spend most of their time at their desks, but make customer visits to close deals or further relationships when the opportunity justifies it. As companies adapt Sales 2.0 practices, there may be a blurring between traditional field sales and Inside Sales roles.

You can use Sales 2.0 practices in your recruiting efforts, too. One company that offers innovative online recruiting solutions is Jobvite. Their product fundamentally changes the way companies hire by incorporating social networking and collaboration into their recruiting application.

IMPLEMENTING SALES 2.0 TRAINING

Sales 2.0 means following a sales process and selling the way your customer is buying. That may not be face-to-face, whether or not your sales organization includes Inside Sales. Josiane Feigon, president of Tele-Smart Communications, specializes in training sales teams and managers on inside selling. She covers the 10 skills sales team members must have (the "TeleSmart 10") in order to successfully engage customers by phone and Web. She says a key to her success is involving a sales team's direct managers and teaching them how to motivate their reps to follow sales process and how to improve results with metrics tracking and coaching.

Geoff Alexander and Company is another well-respected sales training organization with a focus on Inside Sales and related Sales 2.0 principles. Their customized approach considers that sales training for field sales should be conducted differently from sales training for Inside Sales professionals.

STRUCTURING THE RIGHT COMPENSATION

Sales 2.0 companies drive specific behavior and better business results with compensation. In Sales 2.0, there is a shifting emphasis from individual achievement only to individual achievement plus team success plus the success of your customers. Special bonuses or contests, for example, should be motivating to everyone on the sales team, not just the top performers. A contest that has only one winner can quickly be discouraging to those who do not have a chance against someone who can win with one big sale. Sales 2.0 contests and bonuses enable multiple winners or even an entire team to win if the goal is met.

Contests can be run to support the Sales 2.0 process. For example, Witness Systems ran a weekly pipeline-building contest for the tele- sales team, based on the additions to the pipeline and movement of transactions through various sales cycle stages. The results were com- municated weekly to the sales team, including sales managers, regional VPs, and several executives. The VP of sales would congratulate the winner publicly. The winner also received a $250 bonus each week (assuming minimum thresholds were met), which was motivating, but it was the publicity factor that really made the contest effective and competitive in a positive way. As a result, Witness improved the front end of the sales process, as the pipeline grew approximately 25 percent more per week than before the weekly contest began.

Sales 2.0 companies know that offering a competitive and fair com- pensation plan is important to attract the best talent, and they bench- mark their compensation packages with the industry and even their specific competitors when possible. You can track sales compensation for a variety of sales roles via our web site at *www.sales20book.com/resources*.

MOTIVATING SALESPEOPLE WITH COMPENSATION MANAGEMENT SYSTEMS

One account executive we interviewed said, "About half my monthly commission statements, which are calculated using spreadsheets, have errors on them, usually in the company's favor. I spend several hours every month reconciling my statements and correcting these types of errors."

There is nothing more demotivating than messing up salespeople's commissions. And salespeople spending time on correcting compen- sation problems means reduced sales productivity. Sales 2.0 companies recognize the importance of timely and accurate compensation of the sales team. Unfortunately, many organizations still track and reconcile commission payments using spreadsheets and manual processes. As a result, closing the quarter's results and financial statements can take weeks or months, causing compensation delays that can demotivate salespeople.

A number of technologies are available to address this issue, including solutions from Centive, Xactly, and Callidus Software. They provide on-demand sales compensation and performance management solutions that go beyond calculations of sales commissions and bonuses. Executives, sales managers, and salespeople can get real-time visibility into quota attainment, ranking, and commission earnings data. Both Centive and Xactly integrate with salesforce.com and other customer relationship management systems. Both systems enable salespeople and their managers to forecast commission earnings based on opportunities in their pipeline, so they are tied into the Sales 2.0 processes as well.

19

SALES 2.0 PROCESS: DEFINING AND MEASURING YOUR CUSTOMER-CENTRIC SALES STEPS

Sales 2.0 measurability, predictability, and sales science are powered by successful commitment to sales process. But sales process definition needs to start with your customer. One of the hardest things to do when you're faced with a large quota, limited headcount, and a looming end of quarter is to think about sales from your customers' point of view. As sales reps, we have been trained to focus on *our* process, *our* next steps, *our* forecast. Incorporating a focus on the customer into your sales process requires taking the time to ask good questions so you can understand their buying process, and it usually requires you to exercise some flexibility to align with them. When defining and tracking your sales process, you have a number of items to consider.

UNDERSTANDING YOUR CUSTOMERS' EXPERIENCE

An important element to customer focus is understanding the experience a customer or prospect has when engaging with your company. As one way to get the customers' perspective, think about the following questions: Have you ever called into your own company, posing as a prospective customer, or visited your own web site and tried to find product information? Have you requested information online or attempted to engage with a sales rep through IM? How was the experience? Did you get the information you wanted? Was there any follow-up? Were you forced into a communications mode that didn't make sense, such as chat when a phone call would have been more expedient? Give it a try sometime. You might find some areas where you can improve your processes while making it easier for the prospect to do business with you.

TRACKING METRICS IN ADDITION TO REVENUE

Most companies measure sales productivity by one metric: revenue. But without measuring the effectiveness of each stage within the sales process, it is difficult to make corrections mid-quarter to improve results. Sales process measurement is critical to helping sales managers predict team and individual revenue contribution. This level of analysis can help executives make prudent and timely investments in lead generation programs, technology, and training in the event of an anticipated shortfall.

Measuring the effectiveness of each sales process stage is not easy, and measuring it at the individual level is even more difficult, but Sales 2.0 companies know that the results justify the effort. Defining the steps in your sales process according to how your customer buys is a prerequisite. In Part 3, we highlighted Stu Schmidt's contributions to WebEx in the area of sales process definition and measurement and the resulting revenue success. Chapter 13 includes an example of WebEx's customer-centric sales process.

Some customer relationship management (CRM) and other systems are now making sales process measurements and reporting easier for sales management to access. With these advanced technologies, it is now possible to track a vast number of sales metrics, which can be more overwhelming than helpful. To get started with sales process tracking and measurement, focus on a handful of key metrics in the beginning; you can always add more after you've confirmed the basics of your sales process. Some fundamental metrics include total sales cycle length (i.e., how long it takes to close a sale), ASP, and conversion rates from one key sales step to the next, such as your "close rate" from forecast to close.

Let's look at basic sales process measurement in a little more detail, using standard reports from Landslide's sales workstyle management system. The first report (Figure 19.1) analyzes the sales process steps, from Prospect (P) to Qualify (Q), to Consult (C) to Negotiate (N) to Close (C), and tells us the average sales cycle length, by stage, for each salesperson on the same team. The white lines represent transitions from one sales cycle stage to the next, and a light grey area within a given segment shows where that rep lags behind defined benchmarks in that sales cycle phase. We can see that the overall sales cycle length is similar

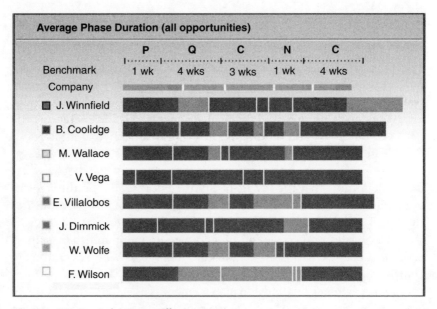

Figure 19.1   Sales Team Effectiveness

for these eight salespeople. We can also understand the average length of time that reps and customers spend at each stage. This company, then, can start to make assumptions based on real data that can help predict the timing and likelihood of future revenue, as it continues to track and verify consistent measurements, such as the lengths of average sales cycles and sales process steps. The report also reveals important data on the individual effectiveness of each sales team member. We can see which salespeople may need help in certain stages of the sales process, based on the average amount of time they are spending in each step. J. Winnfield, for example, has a relatively long prospecting phase, the shortest consult phase but the longest overall sales cycle length, perhaps because too much time was spent prospecting or because the consulting phase was performed hastily. This information helps managers identify team strengths and weaknesses that can be addressed by training, technology, and best-practices sharing to raise overall team performance.

The second report (Figure 19.2) measures the conversion rate of each sales cycle stage for each salesperson. A lower conversion rate

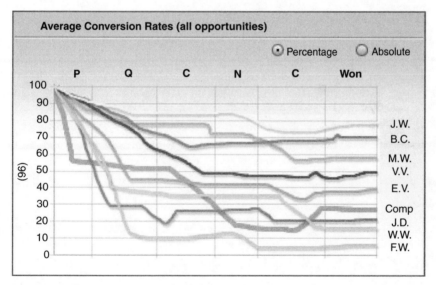

Figure 19.2 Average Conversion Rates

beyond the first stage or two means the salesperson is spending time on opportunities that ultimately do not close. However, a low conversion rate on the first stage is not necessarily a bad thing because in the initial qualification step, unqualified prospects do not progress to the next step in the sales process. Stated another way, if you are going to lose, lose early and spend the rest of your time on opportunities that have the highest probability of closing! On the other hand, a consistently low conversion rate may indicate problems with demand generation marketing program effectiveness, which can lead to an inadequate pipeline of qualified leads. Through measurement of the sales process, you can detect this early.

20

SALES 2.0 TECHNOLOGY: SELECTING THE RIGHT ENABLING TOOLS

An entire book series could be written on the hundreds of technologies that enable Sales 2.0. Instead, we present here an introduction to several key product types and how sales teams are using them to increase productivity and results. We direct you to our web site, *www.sales20book.com/resources*, for future updates on Sales 2.0 technologies that work.

Web 2.0 and other advancements in technology have enabled software vendors to offer their software as a service (SaaS) on a subscription basis, which in turn has allowed customers to pilot new technologies with minimal investments of time and money. As you read this section, we encourage you to remember there is no technology that will make you a Sales 2.0 company, and there are no specific milestones to indicate that you have achieved Sales 2.0 success. However, many of these technologies, which enable the sales practices described throughout this book, can help you produce better business results. Companies that are trying new things to improve sales have achieved our definition of Sales 2.0 success.

Most Sales 2.0 technologies address the key themes of Sales 2.0 by optimizing the efficiency and effectiveness of your sales process, or by helping you develop better relationships, communication, and collaboration. Some technology types, such as CRM or Web Collaboration address multiple Sales 2.0 initiatives. We encourage you to start by focusing on your sales process and your customers' communications preferences, and then evaluating the technologies than can optimize or automate each.

A FUNDAMENTAL: CRM SYSTEMS

One of the most important technologies for the sales organization is customer relationship management (CRM). When it comes to implementing software for the Sales 2.0 organization, CRM is your first priority, as it is the system of record for all the information about your prospects and customers from orders to phone conversations to e-mail addresses, and it is the basis for fundamental sales process measurement. Gartner, Inc., a widely recognized IT market research and consulting firm, identified salesforce.com, NetSuite, Oracle, SAP, and Microsoft as leading CRM vendors, based on their completeness of vision and their ability to execute (Gartner Group, "Magic Quadrant for Salesforce Automation," June 2007).

CRM has been around for more than a decade, but Sales 2.0 companies are using CRM in new and innovative ways. For example, customers are extending their systems to include sales-enabling applications that are integrated with their CRM, and vendors are making it easier to do so. For example, salesforce.com has created the AppExchange, (*www.salesforce.com/appexchange*) a marketplace for on-demand applications that offers hundreds of precertified products built by a community of developers, customers, and partners. One popular AppExchange product is DemandBase, an online service that lets you buy sales leads and create marketing lists on a pay-as-you-go basis, right from within salesforce.com. Irrelevant names and duplicates no longer need to get imported into your salesforce.com system. DemandBase checks against your existing leads and contacts, and removes duplicates. Some of the other vendors mentioned in this chapter (e.g., LucidEra and EchoSign) are also part of the AppExchange community.

Despite all the latest innovations, though, CRM systems often still operate essentially like accounting systems, keeping track of customers, sales, and forecast data. This activity is important for the business, although it does not always improve day-to-day selling for the sales-people themselves. Salespeople acknowledge the efficiency benefits from having their contacts organized and easily accessible, but next-generation CRM systems also focus on sales effectiveness and enable reps to improve their individual sales performance through the buying and selling process.

Landslide Technologies is one company that has addressed this issue by merging CRM technology with sales process optimization. Landslide includes the standard data collection and tracking abilities of most CRM systems, but their product also helps you develop and integrate your unique sales process, or multiple sales processes. Sales and marketing managers can work together to determine which sales tools should be available and recommended by the system for each salesperson based on where they are in the sales process. Landslide also offers a decision makers' portal, a private site enabling salespeople to better gauge prospects' interest levels and connect buying processes with their selling processes. The portal alerts Landslide users in real time when their customers open their documents, who opened them, and if any comments were made.

Teletracking is one company experimenting with a new approach to CRM. Managing sales cycles for Teletracking, a leader in workflow automation solutions for health care, was challenging because of the complexity of selling to hospitals. Each sale required significant sales and presales resources to address the needs of multiple stakeholders involved in the purchase decision. Accurate sales forecasting was a challenge with a decentralized team in which each salesperson followed his or her own method to close deals. Teletracking's CEO, Anthony Sanzo, was looking to increase forecast accuracy and consistency of performance by the sales team. He needed a way to implement a standard selling process for his entire sales team with selling activities and sales support tools based on the best practices for his company. He also wanted to boost the performance of B and C players while helping A players continue to excel in a complex selling environment. Landslide enabled Teletracking to easily define a fully customized sales process complete with sales resources so that the entire sales team was following a consistent approach to customers. As a result, Sanzo's salespeople are now able to manage 25 percent more deals, and they are closing a significantly higher percentage. Forecasting accuracy was also improved, reaching an all-time high of more than 90 percent. Sanzo added, "We needed a product to help facilitate and speed a consistent sales process across our geographically dispersed sales team. With Landslide, our entire sales team could easily adopt and follow a selling process that clearly defined the goals and activities of each selling phase."

Oracle's Social CRM product integrates CRM with social networking technology, which is discussed later in this chapter, to assist salespeople with customer engagement and collaboration. A few examples of how salespeople and managers could use this technology to improve sales effectiveness and efficiency are as follows:

☐   A sales team creates a list of prospects in a specific industry based on ideal customers' previous orders. Leveraging integrated business data from online information source Dun and Bradstreet and the analytics within Oracle, salespeople can access the profiles of other customers or prospects similar to those ideal customers. Salespeople can review the specific buying patterns of those ideal customers and plan a sales strategy based on the new leads' predicted buying behavior.

☐   Your sales team is preparing a presentation for a sales opportunity that includes a new product. The team searches for content available in the system by user rating and relevancy. The system directs the team to the most appropriate content and to the authors of that content if further clarification is needed. The team members can also review previous sales and marketing campaigns (such as webinar or e-mail campaigns) performed by their peers.

☐   A sales team receives a lead in a new industry they have not sold to before. Leveraging the integrated social networking technology, your salespeople can quickly identify friends or colleagues in their network with connections to contacts that industry.

MANAGING PARTNER RELATIONSHIPS: PRM

In Sales 2.0, the sales organization is focused on buyer relationships, which include not only customers and prospects, but also partners. Partner relationship management (PRM) is a business system and strategy for improving communication and collaboration between companies and their partners. PRM applications, often a module within CRM software, allow businesses to better exchange information, manage relationships, and coordinate activity across Sales, Marketing, and Services. Salespeople use PRM software to share prospect information, schedule activities and strategize online, helping to integrate partners with their sales process and lowering the cost of partner sales opportunities.

From a Sales 2.0 management perspective, PRM can help you analyze which partners are most profitable and which need improvement. PRM applications can help you identify and track partner skills and resources so you can match the right partner to the right opportunity. PRM can also automatically route leads to the most appropriate channel partners based on predefined business rules. Most leading CRM vendors offer an integrated PRM application or module.

Riverbed Technology, the market leader in enterprise-class wide-area data services (WDS) solutions, uses salesforce.com's PRM application to forward leads to partners, track joint opportunities, share information and collaborate through the partner portal. M. J. Shutte, Riverbed's Senior Director of Corporate Sales, tells us, "Since a substantial part of our revenue comes through business partners, our channel relationships are clearly critical to our success." The PRM application also allows Riverbed's salespeople and managers to see when a partner accepts a lead and view any of their related notes.

APPLYING BUSINESS INTELLIGENCE TO SALES: SALES ANALYTICS

In the context of Sales 2.0, Business Intelligence (BI) is more than just number crunching by analysts in a back room. Whether you are collecting the data from a BI system, a CRM system, or even spreadsheets, Business Intelligence provides data that leads to actions that improve sales results and productivity. In addition to the sales metrics we discussed in the last chapter, Sales 2.0 leaders are using BI to get measurable answers to strategic questions such as the ones below, and then take appropriate steps based on the information uncovered.

- ☐ How much will we sell this month/quarter/year?
- ☐ Who are our best customers (based on revenue, profit, order size, ongoing business)?

☐   Who are our least profitable customers?

☐   Who are my best salespeople (based on quota attainment, win rates, average discount or profitability, sales cycle times, ability to sell new products, etc.)?

☐   Who are my best partners?

☐   What are my best products (based on sales, profit, growth rate, etc.)?

Armed with the answers to these types of questions, executives can ensure that other parts of the business are scaling in line with the most likely sales results. Frontline sales managers can provide targeted coaching to each salesperson based on his or her strengths and weaknesses. Marketing and product development managers can make investments and activity decisions based on actual sales and forecast data.

Historically, sales managers rarely performed in-depth sales analyses, largely because of the complexity and time required. However, the latest technology advancements are making it easier and faster to obtain this information. LucidEra, for example, provides business intelligence technology on demand. Unlike traditional BI solutions, which are relatively difficult to implement, use, manage, and maintain, BI offered by subscription is accessed easily online. No IT involvement is required by the customer, and there are usually minimal upfront costs. In addition to emerging vendors like LucidEra, some of the traditional BI vendors are offering or planning to offer an on-demand approach, including Business Objects (SAP) and Cognos (IBM).

Difficulty in running reports and gathering information leads not only to wasted time, but more importantly, to less timely identification of problems or potential problems that can be corrected. The following example (see Figure 20.1) illustrates how even small performance deviations away from a goal can lead to significant misses after just a month. In this example, both companies measure key sales-related performance indicators like sales, pipeline growth, leads generated, pipeline movement, presentations delivered, and other activities. The company on the left measures every month, while the company on the right measures the same things every day or week. The company on the right is able to take corrective actions sooner and keep its actual performance in line with their goals.

Eric Johnson, VP of Worldwide Business Operations at Serena (a provider of applications for project and portfolio management), used to

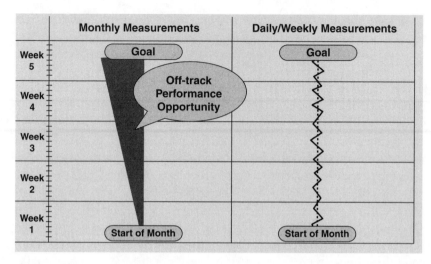

Figure 20.1   Performance Management Tracking

run key performance reports only once a quarter because of the difficulty and time required. One report, for example, measures and filters out just the sales opportunities that have been in a given stage for more than a certain number of days. Eric tells us, "It's a great report for understanding which deals are stalling." As a LucidEra user since January 2008, Serena uses LucidEra's on-demand analytics to improve performance and gain insight that otherwise would have been impossible or difficult to uncover. "And now the same quarterly reports are done in two minutes so they are run every week, enabling appropriate actions to take place at the right time."

GENERATING QUALIFIED LEADS: FINDING THE RIGHT CONTACTS

The ability to identify accurate contacts and leads for your sales and marketing teams has improved dramatically with innovations in web-based technologies. The old, inefficient cold calling in a Sales 1.0 model often meant dealing with lead lists full of obsolete contact information, resulting in a waste of precious selling time. Sales 2.0 companies leverage the Internet to improve their lead generation. We'll discuss two ways they do this: by using their company's web site more effectively as a lead qualification tool, and by using online directories of business contacts to obtain more accurate information for their targeted leads.

The company web site can be a powerful qualifier of inbound leads, when prospects are invited to engage with you online via your web site in various ways. Given the popularity of search technology with buyers, companies of all sizes are spending more of their marketing budget on Google and Yahoo! keyword advertising, in addition to direct response marketing campaigns, to drive traffic to their web sites. In exchange for information of perceived value to buyers, such as podcasts, newsletters, videos, analyst reports, and white papers, you can request that prospects fill out simple forms on your site. These forms allow you to capture information about prospects, such as their company type and size and their title or functional role, as well as their interests. This makes it easier to prioritize and route each lead to an appropriate salesperson, who in turn can follow up with more pertinent messages. Sales 2.0 companies make it easy to interact with their web site visitors through e-mail, live chat, or even a click-to-call feature that can initiate a call through the web connection or to a standard telephone. And some e-mail and web site tracking technologies, discussed in more detail later in this chapter, enable you to proactively interact with your prospects in real time while they are on your web site, as they demonstrate a specific interest in your business.

For outbound lead generation, in addition to leading traditional list providers such as Hoover's, InfoUSA, and ZoomInfo, there are relatively new online services that allow businesspeople to upload and share their contacts with each other. Two popular examples are Spoke and Jigsaw. Spoke incorporates contact information from traditional list vendors and combines that with its own user-validated list data, creating a database of more than 40 million business contacts. In June 2006, Nadine Heintz of *Inc.com* magazine referred to Jigsaw as "the world's biggest Rolodex" (*www.inc.com/magazine/20060601/priority-networking.html*).

Jigsaw has over 450,000 plus members who build and maintain its contact database. Members purchase or trade contact information or online business cards in return for contact information they need. The more contacts you contribute, the more points, or credits, you earn. You also get points when you update incorrect contacts. And if members add bad contacts, they lose points. This innovative business model is proving to be successful, since 450,000 plus members are able to maintain a contact database better than the staff of a single company.

John Fales, Manager of Inside Sales at Bay Area e-mail security provider Post X (which was acquired by IronPort Systems and then by Cisco Systems), has used the Internet extensively to prospect for sales leads. Fales's team has tested Google and other web search engines to find customers but found that approach to be time-consuming and cumbersome. Fales's team also used traditional lead lists from major vendors but found that they were often filled with incomplete or out-of-date information, which led to less efficient prospecting and wasted selling time by his team members. But then Fales learned about Jigsaw. He reports that Jigsaw allows his team to rapidly find decision makers and contract the sales development process when identifying new business opportunities. As a result, his team has generated revenue in the seven-figure range, which Fales credits to Jigsaw. "We've been able to get into accounts very quickly as well as find a variety of potential players in a position to buy our product through the Jigsaw service. It's been consistently helpful. It would be very difficult to go back to the old way."

IMPROVING SALES DEVELOPMENT: EXPEDITING LIVE CONTACTS

With the advent of voice mail, it has become increasingly difficult to reach prospects by telephone. In some industries, it takes seven calls or more to make a live connection. To optimize overall sales efficiency and reduce sales cycle lengths, improving the conversion or connect rate from attempted contact to live connection is a key factor in a sales development campaign or in the early stages of the sales cycle.

ConnectAndSell delivers sales prospects to your salespeople live by phone so they can spend more of their productive time engaging with customers rather than leaving voice mail message after voice mail message. ConnectAndSell can accelerate the process of making live contacts through a combination of patented switching technology and outsourced sales agents. When the sales agents get the prospect on the phone, your salesperson is immediately connected and the prospect believes that your salesperson has made the call; unlike other technologies, such as automatic call dialers, there is no lag time. The ConnectAndSell sales agents never speak to your prospects directly.

According to a CSO Insights poll of over 1,500 companies' sales VPs, the industry average for live conversations with prospects is 0.7 to 1.2 per hour. But Chairman of ConnectAndSell Shawn McLaren, believes his company can do much better. ConnectAndSell guarantees five live connects (i.e., conversations with named individuals you have targeted) to each of your salespeople per hour, and they typically average 7 to 10 per hour. As we are writing this chapter, McLaren reiterated his company's guarantee, stating, "If we don't deliver five live connects per hour to your targeted prospects, you pay nothing."

Sonoa's sales development team was producing 50 live connects per week. Mike Williams, Senior Vice President of Sales for Sonoa Systems (a provider of solutions for securing, managing, and scaling customer-facing Web services for SOA, SaaS, and mash-ups), wanted to do better. He tells us his experience with outsourcing this part of the sales process to ConnectAndSell. Mike says, "I was a naysayer when this concept was originally suggested to me. Based on my experience building and running several lead generation and sales teams, I didn't think ConnectAndSell could deliver on their promise." But there was very little risk with giving them a trial period. Once Sonoa started using ConnectAndSell, the connect rate quickly increased three times to 150 per week. And the conversions to qualified appointments also increased three times, resulting in an additional $200,000 added to the funnel on average every week. Further, since Sonoa is in an emerging market, it benefited from the ability to test more quickly and validate various messages to its target market.

GETTING TO KNOW YOUR CUSTOMER: SALES INTELLIGENCE

Never before has there been so much customer and prospect information so readily available to frontline salespeople. The Internet is changing the way we sell, and it's resulting in the replacement of cold calls with warmer, more personalized calls, as we covered in our discussion of Cold Calling 2.0 in Chapter 9. In addition to making improvements in lead qualification and sales development, reviewed in the last section, salespeople can now leverage the Internet and emerging Sales 2.0 technologies to learn more about their qualified prospects and their specific needs before a sales call.

Those of us who have been in sales for a few years remember the old days when there were just a handful of places to find information about prospects and customers; the challenge then was that too little information was available and it was quite costly. Today just the opposite is true: information is much cheaper (and increasingly is free), but the challenge now is information overload. It is not uncommon to see salespeople with five or more web browsers open just to do basic prospecting and account research. Some emerging Sales 2.0 technology companies have taken notice of this new challenge. Vendors addressing this challenge include Before the Call, Factiva (Dow Jones), and InsideView.

InsideView is a business search and intelligence company that aggregates traditional subscription-based and Web 2.0 user-generated data sources and then uses customizable agents to alert Sales of compelling business events (e.g., leadership changes, new product launches, outstanding RFPs). InsideView's technology also automates the discovery of personal and professional relationships that help salespeople make connections with customers. Its flagship product, SalesView, is considered one of the first examples of what they call a "socialprise" application, bringing together social media and enterprise applications as a mash-up of both the user interface and the information from these previously separate worlds. SalesView taps 20,000-plus data sources, including sites like Hoover's, Reuters, Dun & Bradstreet, ZoomInfo, Facebook, LinkedIn, and Jigsaw, along with web-based news sources, blogs, and job postings to help sales teams automate prospecting, accelerate sales cycles, and ultimately close deals. James Zagelmeyer, executive vice president of Advantage, a talent services firm, states, "With InsideView we have been able to improve the speed and quality of our account research." Advantage credits InsideView with helping to increase its close rate from 10 to 50 percent.

IDENTIFYING CUSTOMER INTEREST: E-MAIL AND WEB SITE TRACKING

Salespeople can gain significant productivity benefits by focusing on the people who are most interested in their products. But how do you know who those people are before investing significant time and money in outbound calling campaigns and qualification calls? Monitoring customer and prospect interest from e-mail responses and web site activity tracking are two effective practices of Sales 2.0 companies. These companies use technology to better understand their customers' interests, before a live interaction takes place, which is particularly useful for the initiation of a personalized, consultative sales process. Since e-mail marketing and company web sites are ubiquitous, virtually any business can benefit from this type of technology. A few leading vendors offering e-mail response and web site activity tracking solutions are Genius.com, iHance, Marketo, and Eloqua.

With products like Genius.com's (profiled in Part 3), you can track your customers' responses to your e-mails and the pages they view on your web site. Leads are routed to the appropriate salespeople in real time, giving them an opportunity to contact the prospect when they are thinking about your company and products, which also increases the connect rate that is directly linked to improving sales productivity. Salespeople spend more time talking with qualified prospects and less time leaving voice mail, navigating through gatekeepers, and following up with prospects who aren't interested in buying.

Eloqua also offers a broad suite of tools for demand generation, lead scoring, and analytics that help businesses automate and measure marketing and lead generation campaigns. Eloqua's prospect-tracking Conversion Suite gives visibility into customer behavior and interests as a result of automated measurements and analytics. By understanding the specific events that trigger desired customer behavior—such as a visitor's Google or Yahoo! search, white-paper downloads, number of visits, time spent on specific pages, or other relevant indicators—businesses can segment these visitors and respond to each in a personalized fashion. That response can be immediate—by engaging them in a proactive online chat, or routing the lead to an Inside Sales team for a follow-up call.

Customers report that the core products from vendors such as genius.com, iHance, Marketo, and Eloqua improve sales productivity. Their sales development groups can optimize their ability to prioritize and follow up on leads. Salespeople benefit by getting warmer leads customers who have already prequalified themselves to some degree. Salespeople know in advance of a call which products are of the most interest and can tailor their selling accordingly. E-mail and web site tracking products are also effective sales and marketing management tools, since their reporting can be used to calculate the effectiveness of various sales messages or promotions.

SPEEDING UP THE APPROVAL CYCLE: ONLINE CONTRACTING

Order forms, master license agreements, statements of work, partner contracts, and nondisclosure agreements are just some of the contracts that are required in most vendor-client relationships. Electronic agreements have existed for several decades, but it was the Federal E-SIGN Act signed in 2000 that facilitated the adoption of e-signatures in a number of industries. As a result of the E-SIGN Act, online e-signatures on commercial transactions are equivalent to written signatures. Similar electronic signature laws have been passed in Europe. Today, thousands of companies use online contracting or e-signatures to reduce their sales cycles.

In addition to facilitating the approval process, online contracting systems store and manage all of your signed agreements as well as those still in the approval process. Many companies still rely on file cabinets with hundreds or even thousands of folders administered by a team of people who act as unnecessary gatekeepers. Meanwhile, users of online contracting can quickly search for specific contracts within seconds. For security and control purposes, rules can be set to limit the amount of access by individual users. And in addition to reducing the length of your sales cycle, online contracting can automate and improve internal processes that require documented approvals.

Silanis and EchoSign are a couple of the leading vendors betting that e-signatures or online contracting will enter the mainstream. EchoSign's process of online contracting is easy: the salesperson (or owner of a document) sends an e-mail and attaches the contract through EchoSign, and the recipient has an option to simply click a button to "e-sign" or print, sign, and fax the document to an EchoSign fax number. EchoSign does the rest. The company tracks all phases of the document signing process, and the user can even schedule automated reminders until a customer signs. Alternatively, EchoSign's system supports a fax signature when a traditional signature is needed. Either way, all parties automatically receive a signed copy of the agreement. EchoSign claims their system helps close $100 million in contracts every month with an average signing time to contract of 42 minutes. Kathy Lord, VP of sales at Intacct, reports, "EchoSign is an absolute must have for any sales team that needs to survive in a Sales 2.0 world. After our initial rollout, our time to signature went from days to just minutes. Our reps and services team have embraced it like a fish to water."

Some electronic signature products like EchoSign offer an optional feature that allows you to cancel a contract that has not been responded to in a certain time frame, and it notifies the recipient that the contract has been cancelled. One large technology vendor reported great success using that feature, especially since a good portion of its contracts included pricing or terms with a stated expiration date. When prospects received a notice saying their contract had expired, many called the vendor back saying, "Wait, we really want it!"

ENGAGING CUSTOMERS: WEB CONFERENCING AND ON-DEMAND PRESENTATIONS

Whether you are conducting a web conference to educate hundreds of prospects, engaging one-on-one with a specific account, or allowing customers to view your presentations on demand, the benefits of web presentations are well documented. In addition to saving the time and cost associated with traveling, web conferences allow you to engage with more people in less time, and customers often prefer to interact this way as well, particularly when it saves them the time and cost of bringing their geographically dispersed people together for an on-site meeting. Web conferencing is one of the most significant Sales 2.0 technologies since it directly aligns with the key Sales 2.0 tenets of enabling better communication and collaboration while at the same time making sales processes more effective and efficient. Vendors of collaboration technologies include market leader WebEx (Cisco), profiled in Part 3, as well as Citrix Online, Microsoft, IBM, and Adobe.

The Internet continues to enable customers to educate themselves, which can accelerate the buying and selling process and your overall sales cycle length. Providing on-demand presentations or demonstrations is another effective way to exchange information and communicate with customers. All of the major web conferencing vendors offer the ability to record presentations and product demonstrations, which can then be hosted on your web site. Though these are rarely a complete substitute for engaging live with your prospects, they do provide the customer with the ability to engage anytime they want, and become more qualified by the time they do engage live with your sales team. This technology addresses the Sales 2.0 mindset of helping customers buy the way they want to, not the way you want them to buy.

Some sales organizations are making web meetings feel more like in-person meetings by giving their salespeople web video cameras so they can simulate the personal nature of a face-to-face meeting while doing an online product presentation. This has advantages over traditional video conferencing since the customer can see salespeople and their presentations simultaneously on one screen. For some customers, showing a human face makes phone and web interactions more personal and increases their engagement and comfort level. Read more about how the WebEx sales organization uses its own products throughout its sales process in Part 3.

Brainshark has an innovative approach to making on-demand presentations interactive and easy to produce. Their customers simply make a phone call to record the audio part of their presentations, which can then be integrated and edited with other on-screen content such as presentation slides or product demonstrations. Unlike some traditional systems, no digital media experts are required. The Brainshark product also measures your customers' interest in your products, based on tracking when and how they view and interact with your recorded presentations. For example, if you have a presentation that includes a voice and/or video presenting your company and products, Brainshark will let you know in real time when someone views it. Brainshark will also tell you how much time viewers spend on each part of your presentation, how they respond to any interactive parts (e.g., questions about their specific needs), and report these activities and interest areas to your salespeople. Products like Brainshark give prospects the flexibility to view presentations on demand, 24/7, on their own schedule.

Barbara Petroff, Business Development Specialist at Siemens Water Technologies Corp. (part of Siemens Corporation), took on the challenge of more effectively presenting products to consultants and potential clients. The need was significant. Before Brainshark, her team spent a great deal of time attempting to describe its complex products in response to numerous phone and e-mail inquiries. Since implementing

Brainshark in 2006, the response to inquiries has been easier and faster, and the message is clearer to the viewer. Barbara explains, "We can direct our clients to our web page where they select the Brainshark link to view a $4\frac{1}{2}$ minute product presentation that is complete with animation and narration. This approach has trimmed hours off of our product introduction efforts and has streamlined the learning process so that we can quickly focus on addressing each client's needs. Having seen our Brainshark presentation, clients can more easily understand the solution that we offer to them. We are spending less time explaining our product and investing more time listening to and assisting our clients. In the first year of use, the Brainshark presentation more than quadrupled the number of clients reached. It would have been impossible to reach that many individuals in the conventional way we functioned before. Brainshark really has changed the way in which we communicate with our clients."

IMPROVING COMMUNICATION AND COLLABORATION: WIKIS, BLOGS, COMMUNITIES, AND SALES PORTALS

Wikis, blogs, online communities, and sales portals are Web 2.0 technologies that provide value to the sales organization by enabling better communication, engagement, and collaboration with customers, prospects, and internal colleagues, thus creating stronger relationships with prospects and customers.

Wikis are often used to create collaborative web sites because anyone in the community, not just authors, has the ability to create and edit web page content. Wikis can be made public or private. One useful application for wikis in the sales function is in intranets (internal Internet), where they can be used as a central repository of information to which salespeople or managers can post and share notes about customer successes, competition, best practices, or links to useful resources. This approach takes the management off the manager or sales operations person who would normally have to administer this kind of web site, though some users of this technology report that managed or moderated wikis provide more value than those without structure or a content review process.

Leads360, a company that specializes in lead management solutions for companies with sales teams that sell direct-to-consumer, uses wikis in its sales process. The company is engaging with its prospects on wikis, and then inviting them to review, edit, and share information. In early 2008, Leads360 implemented a new sales process that was designed with the customer in mind. Emphasizing transparency, the system includes sharing salespeople's edited notes with prospects online, through wikis. After a phone call with a new prospect, a salesperson writes up a matter-of-fact, one- to two-page, password-protected business proposal. The salesperson shares the wiki with the prospect, who can then review it to confirm, correct, or edit the content. Prospects can also easily share this business case with their colleagues, who may be part of the buying process.

Blogs are another online information source that can be used internally to enhance communication and information sharing among employees within a corporation or externally for marketing, branding, or public relations purposes. A blog gives your company a voice, and external blogs give prospects another way to get to know you as they evaluate your company.

Although it's common to think of blogs as lead generation tools, companies using blogs as part of their marketing strategy report that they generally do not generate many new leads. However, blogs are valuable for other reasons. Blogs allow interested parties, including prospects who aren't ready to purchase today, to monitor what the company has to say and to keep in touch. Prospects reading your blog are educating themselves before they ever call you, reducing the amount of time salespeople and prospects need to spend reviewing basic information. For example, Josiane Feigon, who writes the Life in the Telebusiness Trenches blog (*www.tele-smart.com/blog*) says, "People working on improving their sales productivity are often referred to me for help with training. I find that most of them spend some time on my blog, so by the time we talk, we have much more productive conversations."

Online communities, a combination of forums, chat, blogs, and other social networking tools, enable customers and prospects to better communicate and collaborate with each other or with the vendor. This technology, available from companies such as Lithium Technologies and Mzinga, can have an impact on buyer engagement with all functional areas of a business. Although communities are currently most prevalent for customer-service-related activities, they can positively impact sales and marketing, too. They can be used to increase traffic to a company's main web site, resulting in more inbound leads for the sales team. Salespeople can gain important insight by searching for comments made by their targeted customers or prospects. Sales and marketing managers as well as executives benefit by having greater access to the true voice of the customer, which can be acted upon faster than information received only through quarterly surveys or anecdotal feedback from customer service, support, and salespeople. Online communities offer a relatively inexpensive solution to enhancing customer relationships and gaining insight that can be measurably tied to increasing revenue and improving customer retention.

Online communities are often moderated by the vendor (e.g., to manage problem users and inappropriate language), but they generally allow participants to openly give and receive feedback, ideas, requests, and solutions. Communities can also be a great self-service solution as customers often answer questions for each other, improving productivity for vendors by reducing their workload. The risk of not hosting a community site for your customers and prospects is that the market may create one for you, outside of your control or influence. For example, the Yahoo! directory lists over 300 consumer opinion sites that attack major corporations. Many of those users could have been better served at a community site hosted by the company in question, and their public displays of aversion could have been mitigated sooner with the right response.

Some online community sites, such as the one hosted by salesforce.com (*http://success.salesforce.com/*) enable customers to suggest product ideas as well as rate the ideas of others. End users can help shape the product road map like never before. Sales, marketing, and product development leaders can then see what customers really want, in real time, and how much demand there would be for specific products or services. That is valuable information to have *before* engaging in the development and promotion of new offerings.

Although the anecdotal feedback for online communities looks very positive, the specific impact that communities have on sales can vary from company to company. A relatively easy way to measure the financial result is to compare customers' spending before and after their involvement in the online community. One large company in the financial industry reported that sales from online community members increased approximately 41 percent since the community's inception. And in another study, eBay reported that its online community members buy and sell significantly more than noncommunity members.

Gerhard Gschwandtner, Founder and Publisher of *Selling Power* magazine, tells us, "Today it is not enough just to listen to the customer to diagnose needs with the intent to close a sale. What's needed today is to stimulate, facilitate, and enhance conversations with the intention to create a wider and deeper connection that leads to a process of co-creating a better future. Take a look at *mystarbucksidea.com, dellideastorm.com,* and *ideas.salesforce.com.* In the past, companies created customers; in the future, customers will create companies. Customer ecosystems management will lead us into the future."

Sales portals make sales-related tools and documentation more readily available to the salespeople and customers when they need it most, which increases the productivity of the sales organization. From our collective personal experience, we know that many companies and salespeople still use e-mails with attachments to communicate information internally and to customers. The content quickly becomes outdated and it is difficult to retrieve. It is still often left up to the individual salespeople and their customers to efficiently store, organize, and maintain information.

Some companies attempt to solve this problem with a simple intranet site that hosts sales and marketing files. But there is a difference between a true sales portal and an intranet site. Although there are some similarities, sales portals are more advanced. Their content is centrally maintained with version and editing controls, ensuring the latest and most relevant materials are being used to support sales opportunities. They are easier to use and often have advanced, full-text search that shortens the time needed to find the right document. Some sales portals even allow users to rate the content, helping salespeople quickly find the best sales tools for their specific situation.

Sales portals, such as those offered by WebEx and Oracle, also engage other parts of the organization and support several of the key Sales 2.0 imperatives. For example, sales portals enable sales process consistency through the use of the best sales tools at the right stage in the sales process. The sales process itself may be published and maintained through the sales portal, and the use of public ratings can increase the probability that successes using certain tools will be duplicated by other users. Sales portals also foster better communication and collaboration while at the same time offering users the self-service ability to get what they want, when they want it. And perhaps best of all, sales portals increase sales productivity by allowing salespeople to spend less time finding the right information and more time selling.

MAKING STRONGER CONNECTIONS: SOCIAL NETWORKING

Are you more likely to answer an e-mail or take a phone call from someone you don't know or from someone who is a friend of a friend? Social networking technology gives us a tool to discover how we might be connected to someone who is likely to be interested in our products. A warm introduction is always preferable to cold calling to prospect lists, and social networking allows you to make connections through personal referrals. LinkedIn, one of the most popular social networking sites for businesspeople, lets users establish relationships by asking colleagues or friends who are also LinkedIn members to join their networks. Members can search for people based on their name, title, company, or location. Ryze, Plaxo, SaleSpider.com, and Hoover's also offer social networking services for finding business-oriented connections. Some companies are even experimenting with social-networking sites such as Facebook, Ziggs, and Ning that have been more oriented to personal relationships but may in the future become part of the mainstream in business.

Kathleen Bruno, a business development executive at SpikeSource, formerly ran sales at a social networking company, Visible Path, which was acquired by Hoover's in January 2008 and was integrated into the Hoover's Connect product. One of her favorite illustrations of the power of social networking involved a sales opportunity that required her to gain sponsorship from an executive named Bill, who sat on the board of one of the largest high-tech companies in North America. He was guarded by an array of assistants and managers, and penetration to the inner circle seemed almost impossible, even though she was normally successful in getting through to most executives. With the help of her social networking solution, she found a pathway to this executive through one of her board members, who responded to her request for an introduction with the following response: "Yes, I know Bill quite well. In fact, I will be with him at a conference tomorrow in Orlando and will not only make an introduction for you, but will demo the software as well."

Discussion took place in Orlando. Demo completed. Highest level of executive sponsorship gained. Sales cycle collapsed by orders of magnitude. Deal done. Kathleen claims, "Colleagues and friends who are networked together are generally very aligned in supporting each other's efforts and successes."

In addition to finding key people through your social network, there are other benefits to salespeople using social networking. For example, maintaining an online profile page that you share with customers or prospects before your calls or meetings enables them to see what you look like and learn more about you personally (i.e., your previous companies, previous roles, personal interests), which can help you establish credibility or common ground to get the conversation rolling. Social networking sites also allow salespeople to keep their online Rolodex of contacts current automatically as users update their own profiles.

CLOSING COMMENTS: THE FUTURE OF SALES 2.0

Many companies are just beginning to see the results of consistent, dedicated use of Sales 2.0 principles. They will be transforming their sales practices to produce improved business results by strategically aligning their sales organizations with their customers; implementing dynamic sales processes; creating better ways to form long-term, engaging relationships; and evaluating how new technologies support these initiatives. There will be a continuing evolution in communications and how we relate, which will have an effect on how customers buy in the future. We can only imagine the new ways customers and salespeople will engage in the future, as customers become more empowered and online information and relationships become more robust and widespread. What we can be certain of is that Sales 2.0 companies will keep evolving and finding better ways to stay ahead of the competition and produce superior business results.

In the words of Willis Turner, President and Chief Executive Officer of Sales and Marketing Executives International, "Sales 2.0 is real and showing a lot of growth and promise for companies in many industries where innovative technology and processes are being implemented. Professional selling is evolutionary and individuals who embrace Sales 2.0 tools on both sides of the selling equation will enhance productivity as they push the boundaries of this frontier."

AFTERWORD

Sustainable competitive advantage—how we gain an advantage over our competition and then how we sustain that competitive advantage over time—can (and should) come from sales just as it can from other areas of a business. As you've read this book, you've seen the ways sales can improve effectiveness, efficiency, predictability, and results. Centering these improvements on your customer and how your business delivers value to your customer creates your competitive advantage.

Sustaining that competitive advantage means staying one step ahead of your competition. We often hate to admit it, but there is very little we can do to create competitive advantage that our competition can't imitate, and often very quickly. Staying a step ahead requires not only taking at least some of the steps outlined in this book, but continuing to take steps. The ability to take a step and then take another (and another) is how you sustain your advantage.

This is why success in Sales 2.0 requires two critical capabilities in your organization. First, you must be able to create strategy and manage people, process, and technology from a customer-centric point of view. This means looking at what is valuable to your customer and then bringing that back into your strategy and processes. Second, you must keep moving forward. You must continually take steps to improve your selling organization and develop an innovation pipeline to help you try new ideas and use what works best.

The first time I gave a talk about Sales 2.0, the first question from an astute member of my audience was, "Doesn't the emergence of Sales 2.0 imply that there is a Buyer 2.0 out there?" The answer, of course, is yes. A lively conversation ensued about how and when this Buyer 2.0 might emerge and when sales organizations needed to be prepared.

The conclusion was unanimous: Buyer 2.0 is already here and, in fact, has been for a while. It's just been hard for many companies to see the changes that have happened in buying patterns and preferences, and adapt to them quickly enough.

You've read throughout this book about companies that have done well in seeing and understanding new buying patterns and developing innovative new sales practices and processes not only to adapt to this new buyer but also to create strong competitive advantage for themselves by helping their customers buy the way their customers *want* to buy.

The companies that have been the pioneers of Sales 2.0 have seen their business results improve, their customer relationships become stronger, their ability to adapt to ever-changing market conditions increase, and their competitive advantage widen.

The Sales 2.0 evolution is still in its infancy, but the imperative for sales organizations to evolve is not. Buyers' expectations have already changed. They expect more from you, and they expect it faster than ever. Plus, your buyers expect you to find new ways to serve their needs. They expect you not just to pitch your products and solutions, but to help them find ways to use your products to create business results for them and their companies. And while we can only imagine what our buyers will expect of us next, we can be certain it will continue to change, and at an ever-increasing pace.

The Sales 2.0 evolution will also happen faster for companies that succeed in focusing on their customer. From a sales perspective, this means truly hearing customers, not just listening to them. It means focusing on and adapting to the buyer's process, while addressing the needs of the people involved in that process. It means recognizing that buyers have more power and knowledge than ever before, and therefore the role of the sales rep is changing from educator/presenter of information to facilitator of achieving business results. Customer centricity in sales also means selling *and delivering* the expected business results, which requires a closer ongoing relationship beyond the initial purchase to ensure the customer achieves those business results.

When you take steps to improve your people, process, technology, and strategy, you must put yourself in the shoes of your buyer. When you consider experimenting with new ideas, look at them from your buyers' point of view and ask yourself: Does this help my buyer? How does it create value? If you can answer those questions clearly, you're well along the road to creating a customer-centric organization.

Making the Sales 2.0 evolution happen in your organization requires that you start to make changes, but making changes can be scary and is often met with resistance. Many executives and sales leaders see the sales process as, to borrow a phrase from the political pundits, "the third rail of business." The sales process can't be touched, they might say, as it produces the revenue that is the lifeblood of the company, and we can't put that at risk. This leaves the Sales 2.0 executive with an important question: how do I start to change and evolve without putting my revenue engine at risk?

The answer starts with experimentation. This book has offered no shortage of ideas and suggestions on how to become a Sales 2.0 organization. You might not be able to do them all at once, but taking steps—likely small steps at first, and then bigger steps—will get you moving along the path to Sales 2.0.

Experimentation is one of the things leading companies have done successfully for years. Companies that have learned this lesson figured out that not every process, not every procedure, and not every policy needs to be implemented company-wide all at once. They've also learned that trying something new on a small scale allows them to learn how well the new thing worked. They could discard ideas that didn't work very well, improve upon ideas that had promise, and expand and roll out ideas that proved to work well.

The advent of Web 2.0 technologies and Software-as-a-Service (SaaS) now allows companies of all sizes to try technology-enabled experiments in their processes on a small scale, and to try several different approaches to determine what works best. The result is that it's easier than ever to experiment with new ideas, new processes, and new approaches, and to try several different experiments at once to see which works best for you and your organization.

The ongoing shift in technology also allows scaling of relationships like never before. Part of the reason we've historically become much more deeply engaged with only a small number of our customers (typically between 1 percent and 20 percent) is simply that there are limits to our human abilities to focus on developing these relationships. But that leaves 80 percent or more of your customers with little attention from you and much more vulnerable to being stolen by the competition. Leveraging the SaaS and Web 2.0 technologies discussed in this book, we now have the ability to handle many more relationships and keep in regular touch with even those prospects with whom we have the most tenuous of relationships. Success in the world of Sales 2.0 is not just interacting in new ways, but scaling our ability to interact while maintaining a personalized relationship with each customer.

Throughout this book, you've read a wide range of ideas, suggestions, checklists, and things to do to help your sales organization create the outstanding business results promised by the Sales 2.0 transformation. Each of these are things we know work in many sales organizations, and are things you can do tomorrow morning to start making your own Sales 2.0 transformation.

Underlying all the things you can do to begin (or advance) your Sales 2.0 transformation are two important principles. First, everything you do must start with your customer's needs and preferences, and you must bring those needs back into your organization to define your sales strategy and determine how you evolve. Second, you must continue to evolve. Your customers are not standing still, and neither are your competitors.

We know that there is no endgame—no Sales 2.0 Nirvana to achieve. Sales 2.0 is based on experimentation and continuous improvement. The experiments that work become the ones that improve your sales organization. The ones that don't, you just discard and try something else.

The key to continuous improvement is to have your own experimentation pipeline—small customer-centric things you can keep trying and either discard or grow. Like the manufacturing companies that successfully implemented *kaizen* (continuous improvement), becoming a Sales 2.0 organization requires that you keep growing, keep changing, and keep improving, so you can stay one step ahead of your competition and one step closer to your customer.

There is no point at which you can declare that you have become a Sales 2.0 organization, because the true definition of a Sales 2.0

organization is that you've taken one step today beyond the one you took yesterday.

So now go and take a step.

—Jeff Weinberger
Sales 2.0 Marketing Strategist, Cisco WebEx
http://disruptivemarketing.jeffweinberger.com

SALES 2.0 RESOURCES

B ecause Sales 2.0 is always evolving and new, innovative products and services emerge every day, please visit our web site at *www.sales20book.com/resources* for the most current information and web sites links.

If you are a supplier of Sales 2.0 products or services and would like to be included on our web site, please contact us at *www.sales20book.com*.

The companies mentioned in the book include:

Strategy

Sales 2.0 and Sales Strategy and Implementation Consulting

☐ Phone Works

Sales Effectiveness Research

☐ CSO Insights

People

Recruiting

☐ Corporate Dynamix
☐ Jobvite

Sales Training

- ☐ Corporate Visions, Inc.
- ☐ Geoff Alexander and Company
- ☐ InfoMentis, Inc.
- ☐ M3 Learning
- ☐ TeleSmart Communications, Inc.
- ☐ WINNING, Inc.

Sales Candidate Profiles

- ☐ Caliper
- ☐ Profiles International
- ☐ Sales Judge

Compensation Management

- ☐ Callidus Software
- ☐ Centive
- ☐ Xactly

Process

- ☐ Landslide

Technology

CRM Systems and Integrated Sales Productivity Applications

- ☐ Landslide
- ☐ Microsoft
- ☐ NetSuite
- ☐ Oracle
- ☐ SAP
- ☐ salesforce.com

Sales Analytics

- ☐ Business Objects (SAP)
- ☐ Cloud9 Analytics
- ☐ Cognos (IBM)
- ☐ LucidEra

Finding the Right Contacts/Expediting Live Contacts/Sales Intelligence

- ☐ Before the Call
- ☐ ConnectAndSell
- ☐ DemandBase
- ☐ Factiva (Dow Jones)
- ☐ Hoover's
- ☐ InfoUSA
- ☐ InsideView
- ☐ Jigsaw
- ☐ Spoke
- ☐ ZoomInfo

E-mail and Web Site Tracking

- ☐ Eloqua
- ☐ Genius.com
- ☐ iHance
- ☐ Marketo

Online Contracting

- ☐ EchoSign
- ☐ Silanis

Web Conferencing and On-Demand Presentations

- ☐ Adobe
- ☐ Brainshark
- ☐ Citrix online

- ☐   IBM
- ☐   Microsoft
- ☐   Oracle
- ☐   WebEx (Cisco)

Communities, Sales Portals

- ☐   Lithium Technologies
- ☐   Oracle
- ☐   Mzinga
- ☐   WebEx (Cisco)

Social Networking

- ☐   Facebook
- ☐   Hoover's
- ☐   LinkedIn
- ☐   Ning
- ☐   Plaxo
- ☐   Ryze
- ☐   SaleSpider.com
- ☐   Ziggs

INDEX

233